SELECTED POEMS

BOOKS BY PAUL McLOUGHLIN

with Smith/Doorstop:
What Certainty is Like (1998)

with Shoestring Press:
What Moves Moves (2004)
Forgetting to Come In (2007)
The Road to Murreigh (2010)
The Hungarian Who Beat Brazil (2017)

with Paekakariki Press:
Breaking Ground: The Anglo-Saxon Chronicle Poems in Old English and in Translation (2018/19)

Also with Shoestring Press:
Paging Doctor Jazz (by Various) 2004
Wood & Ink (on Alan Dixon Woodcuts) 2013
Brian Jones: New & Selected Poems (2013)
    (Edited & with Introductory Essay)

with Severn Press:
Whatever Else You Might Say (2021)
Is This Like a Poem (2022)

PAUL McLOUGHLIN: SELECTED POEMS

Edited with an introduction by John Forth

All rights reserved. No part of this work covered by the copyright herein may be reproduced or used in any means – graphic, electronic, or mechanical, including copying, recording, taping, or information storage and retrieval systems – without written permission of the publisher.

Printed by imprintdigital
Upton Pyne, Exeter
www.digital.imprint.co.uk

Typesetting and cover design by The Book Typesetters
hello@thebooktypesetters.com
07422 598 168
www.thebooktypesetters.com

Published by Shoestring Press
19 Devonshire Avenue, Beeston, Nottingham, NG9 1BS
(0115) 925 1827
www.shoestringpress.co.uk

First published 2024
© Poetry: Paul McLoughlin
© Introduction: John Forth
© Cover painting: 'Gull at Slea Head' by Paul McLoughlin
© Author photograph: Nina McLoughlin

The moral right of the author has been asserted.

ISBN 978-1-912524-47-1

ACKNOWLEDGEMENTS

Shoestring Press is grateful to the editors of the following publications where poems or versions of them appeared:
Ambit; Critical Survey; Cyphers (Ireland); Envoi; The Frogmore Papers; Hard Times (Germany); The Interpreter's House, London Grip (online); Magma; Other Poetry; P. N Review; The Rialto; Seam; Smith-Doorstop Books; Smith's Knoll; Southword (Ireland); Tears in the Fence; Wandering Dog

The pamphlet *What Certainty is Like* won publication in the Poetry Business Competition (1997). 'Flugel' appeared in *Paging Doctor Jazz* (Shoestring Press, 2004) and 'The End of Goodbyes' won second prize in the *New Writer* competition of that year. We're grateful to Helen Tobin for providing the translation of the Gaelic rhyme that forms its epigraph.

Thanks also to Nina and Thomas McLoughlin for providing access to computer files containing Paul's poems.

CONTENTS

The Poems of Paul McLoughlin (1947–2021)   1

from *What Certainty is Like* (1998); *What Moves Moves* (2004); *Is This Like a Poem?* (2022); *Forgetting to Come In* (2007)

The Bridge	11
Avancez!	12
Before the Managers Came	13
Marksburg	14
Hope for Hounslow	15
The Men in Their Lives	17
Bouteille	19
Time and Place	21
Marry	22
Father's Brother, Paddy-Joe	23
Home	24
Nicking the Church Lead	27
Another Break-in	29
Whatever Mick Wants	31
Story	32
Anyway and Anyway	33
Sanary-Sur-Mer	34
The Act of Uniformity	35
Four Ways of Looking at A Cabinet	37
The Bicycle Garden	38
Christina's World	39
Hand-Me-Ups	40
Pressing	41
Sky Woman in New York	42
Among the Doublegangers	43
The Grey Dog of Swordland	44
Whistling	45
Know What I Mean?	46
That Was A Way of Putting It	47
What Certainty is Like	48

At the Watermans	49
Fragments of Humanity	51
Children of the Sun	52
Philistine	53
Grouch	54
Channel Hopping	55
Birds	57
Flugel	58
On Magritte's 'Man of the Sea' (1926)	59
Going	60
There's Always This	61
The Good Catholic	62
Margaret by the Fire	63
First Flight	64

from *The Road to Murreigh* (2010)

Firstlings	67
Having the Gift	68
The Noise	69
Mother in Murreigh	70
A Little Treat for James	71
Fishing Rights	72
Maire De Barra	73
Dún an Óir	75
The End of Goodbyes	76
More Than a Myth	80
James is Failing	82
Green and Gold	85
The Road to Murreigh ('Moor-ee-uck')	86
Holy	89
The Long Sticks	91
Hanafin's Mule	92
The Bed and Breakfast History Man	93
Dunquin	94
The Last	96
Stories by the Fire	97
Dingle Nightcap	99
Cró na Snáthaide	100

Ballyluskey	102
Kilmalkedar	103
Safety First	104
Clarke's Windows	105
Lest	106

from *The Hungarian Who Beat Brazil* (2017); *Whatever Else You Might Say* (2021); Uncollected Poems (2018–21)

Mantles	111
Two-O-Eight	112
Brothers	113
Sundays	114
Want	115
The Hungarian Who Beat Brazil	116
The End of Empire	118
House	119
In Praise of Drab	120
Dying Out	122
Ends Meet	123
Ritual	124
Looking for the Boston Lowell	126
Past Passing	127
Gone & Done	128
The Chill Pill	130
Don Cherry	131
How Capitalism Works	132
In Other Words	133
'It's Respect for the Fucking Dead'	134
To Whom It May Concern	135
No Ordinary Clipper	136
Wanted	137
Overnighting	138
The Pier Visitor Experience Manager	139
Shepp	140
Turning Hands	141
The Twentieth Century	142
What They Were Good At	143

NOTE ON PUBLICATIONS

There are three groups of poems comprising:

(1) *What Certainty is Like* (1998); *What Moves Moves* (2004); *Is This Like a Poem?* (2022); *Forgetting to Come In* (2007)

(2) *The Road to Murreigh* (1995–2010)

(3) *The Hungarian Who Beat Brazil* (2017); *Whatever Else You Might Say* (2021); Uncollected Poems (2018-21)

He also contributed to *Wood & Ink* – poems on woodcuts by Alan Dixon – and completed a translation of the Anglo-Saxon Chronicle poems entitled *Breaking Ground* (Paekakariki). These poems are best accompanied by their woodcuts and originals and so are not included here.

THE POEMS OF PAUL McLOUGHLIN
(1947–2021)

A Personal View

Paul and I attended different London Grammar Schools in the 'sixties, both of us having an experience and missing the meaning. There were similarities in our backgrounds too, with parents who missed out on education during the war but who were keen to support us in strange territory. By the time he was sixteen Paul had fought his way out of school and a potential career in the church, whereas I stayed on into the sixth form by the skin of my teeth. Although Paul was three years my senior he began his degree at Borough Road College just as I was leaving it in 1975, and it was here that we met later in the M.Ed evening class having become teachers in comprehensive schools. So there we were in 1978 with a near identical set of memories and teachers from our courses. What follows is not a critique of his poems, but a few snapshots from the time.

Herbert Lomas, who taught us Poetry, later said in a review that 'Paul McLoughlin makes his level-headed bewilderment resound like discovery', and I doubt if anyone described the work more succinctly. We were developing the courage of our lack of convictions. One of our earliest derived from a TV feature, 'One Pair of Eyes', about Tom Stoppard's early plays and preoccupations. It was before any video recording, but I recall a man in a strange raincoat clutching an errant peacock and fleeing his pursuers in an ordinary street, the film-maker suddenly asking Stoppard, who was driving him along the M4, 'What was that?'. Stoppard's reply, a refrain throughout the short film, was 'I don't know'. Later he would add, 'I think I'm beginning to know the M4'. *After Magritte* was part of our wallpaper. We were young men, and celebrating not knowing was Damascan news. Certainties were crowding in, needing to be opposed, and we knew that complex scenarios often have simple explanations, even when we can't know what they are. We'd have proper jobs at last.

Bertie Lomas was referring to pamphlets from Smith-

Doorstop (1998) and Shoestring Press (2004) – a total of 41 poems emerging over six years with some dated earlier. Since these would have made an excellent first collection you wouldn't need Inspector Hound to tell you that 'bewilderment' described Paul's approach to many things, including his CV.

There was no Ireland to hurt him into poetry since he never lived there, but there was residual anger directed against his Catholic schooling. It was seldom explicit – translated perhaps into the 'bewilderment' seen by Bertie Lomas or into a kind of detachment (sometimes called 'ironic'). It resurfaced later as rage that bothered him and kept him awake, a profound oppositional stance that surprised him in its intensity. Usually his target would be the media, politicians and pundits with their talk-talk, footballers who don't play the game…or anyone peddling certainties. But he'd bury rage in deliberate wit or unconcern – setting it up to be knocked down – and the resulting ambivalence was similar to that in the early poems, even as it became more overt. In fact the types of poem that became trademarks later on were all in *What Certainty is Like* – with its range of personae such as the guide to the castle at 'Marksburg'; the restaurant chef in 'Before the Managers Came' (probably father-in-law Rene); the skeptic tip-toeing his way through strange beliefs in 'Hope for Hounslow' and the young man shedding rituals in 'Nicking the Church Lead'. Yet the voice dominating these poems is of an exile. Poems of Ireland such as 'Mother in Murreigh', 'The Noise', 'Fishing Rights', 'Home', 'Father's Brother Paddy Joe' and 'Time and Place' prepare us for his later 'Irish' collection (the first three get a reprise there) but all of them promised other kinds of development too. The seventeen poems in the first pamphlet were chosen from a significant body of work, much of it collected in *Is This Like a Poem?* (2022). I suspect he began with an assurance he never recognised. For one thing, a bushel can disguise the brightness of a light, and anyway he was more experienced than most beginners when he began.

An early poem from the 2022 collection, 'That Was a Way of Putting It' is a case of the 'understated portentous', if that's not too portentous. It was the earliest McLoughlin poem I saw and almost certainly among his very first:

> Between the whistle which you did not hear
> and the whistle which you will not hear
> there are corners, a time for repossession.
> Not turning points for there is no turning
> but moments when the ball is still.

'What Certainty is Like' from the same collection is an early poem so why does it look like a late one? Was it Peter Sansom or Paul himself who decided not to publish? I'm going with a not guilty plea, though I may have had a hand in it, but it was likely held back by some earlier forced endings. This version has an ending that works:

> Why risk tanked-up rough-houses asking
> what your problem is when you can give nothing
> a chance to happen and then have all night
> to set about them in the dark.

The second pamphlet collection, with Shoestring, was called *What Moves Moves* (2004), the title coming from its end poem 'Know What I Mean' which grapples with simple misnomers like 'earthrise' on the grounds that it doesn't. Before this, 'Among the Doublegangers' is one of several poems in which Paul seemed fated to meet people who either directly resembled him or who went under the same name. A poem about a burglary in which a valuable sax was missed by the perps describes investigator PC Bradley asking the usual questions in a laid back narrative ('Another Break-in'). A woman in war smothers her child while trying to hide, finishing up on both sides of the conflict ('Story'), and a circus performer embraces ambivalence: 'When she was sawn in half she could choose/ the roads not taken' ('Anyway and Anyway'). These characters have what Peter Carpenter called 'felt life'.

The people of Eyam who self-isolated in 1665 to prevent the spread of plague ('The Act of Uniformity') were similarly substantial, along with 'Christina's World', where a reference to Bartok's music revealed Paul's tendency to wear arts lightly. But the manifesto, should we seek one, comes in a poem to his brother, Mick:

> Your tenor sax speaks jazz with the same
> lazy filling up of space
> you lead everyone to think you'll leave unfilled.

Like Mick's jazz, these poems achieve their effects, their clarity, with unforced skill. 'Know What I Mean?' ends the book and clarifies what Paul meant by clarity. Poeticised concepts such as 'earthrise' in photos taken from the moon show Stoppard's 'Jumpers' hanging around long after its mission returned. What moves moves. If it moves it moves. If it doesn't move why are you telling me it does? It was hard work sometimes.

The first full collection had been teasingly titled *Forgetting to Come In* (2007). For the jazzman this would be a significant embarrassment of course. For others, the customary bewilderment is there in the forgetting, and having to 'come in' sounds like an instruction to conform or, from a parent, a distraction or constraint. You'd be joining something. So forgetting is deliberate. In 'Round Midnight', a part of 'At the Waterman's' (near the M4) we're reminded of what a rockstar said when Coltrane died – that it was 'a shame / he never made it'. So what's the point of 'remembering'? A terrifying mock-jazz outfit from a Holbein woodcut is foregrounded in 'Fragments of Humanity' and in 'Children of the Sun' poets are reluctantly given jobs by the gutter press:

> Agreed, it isn't wise to turn down
> anyone with a degree
> of aptitude and I admit they can
> write, but poets have no
> stomach for the elasticity of
> truth we're looking for.

Since 'no self-respecting writer'd/ get out of bed for what a poet/calls an audience', you'd be forgiven for calling time on the poetry game. Finally poets earn a place on 'the Subs bench' since they are, 'reliably grammatical, / and some can spell'. The book is of would-be escapees at the start of 'the Brian Jones period', and the eye is drawn to 'Grouch' or the grunt: 'My father / grunted, and I've been fighting him off /since then'.

Paul learned from Jones that if we stick around long enough, 'we'll only turn into / the selves who stuck around… knowing / where they're going is where they are'. It's an unforgiving mantra that may console as well as depress. In a group of 'shorts' directed at TV and called 'Channel Hopping' the speaker identifies a need to avoid irony ('a cheap / way out of facing up to life…') The News and a wildlife programme are presented in uneasy marriage where a bear thinks she's human: 'Perhaps there's / something in us she can see'.

It felt like *The Road to Murreigh* (2010) had been waiting in the wings when it appeared. Three poems are from the first pamphlet (1998) and 'The End of Goodbyes' opened the first full collection (2007). Paul wrote about the West of Ireland with all the love possible short of actually wanting to live there. One of his characters had said *O, but it's better than the noise*, and I'm sure he felt that too, and maybe nostalgia is tweaked like that anyway – dreaming something we can't want. In a short preface, he wrote: *It is the place that registers with me, because I have never harboured any real interest in family history.* Surely the family history he dismisses is the bureaucratic one, since place and people charm him in the poems. Time and again, especially in the speech of Uncle James, local idioms translate as beauty. The first two poems refer to a visit with his family in 1952, when he was five and baby Mick kept breaking bottles on the stone floor. His mother 'disappeared' to the ceilidh on the strand where she danced with the local garda and later miscarried a pregnancy he wouldn't have known about.

Without a supernatural bone in body or mind, Paul forever puzzled about his strange ability to picture the family cottage before he'd seen it. Even deja vu would have scientific explanations of course, but he was astounded by the accuracy of a 'memory' of something unseen. It plays out in the poems as a counterpart to his mother's dementia, which became an unwanted vehicle conveying a past she couldn't have access to:

> For the umpteenth time you ask
> contrary James how many
> sugars has he in his tea. The smile
> he shakes his head with's meant for me.

('Mother in Murreigh')

There are many poems that evoke a sense of mystery about the place, but 'Fishing Rights' is unusual in the way it presents topsy-turvy as completely natural:

> Armada Spanish hid in these hills and changed their names.
> Had they stayed at home till Franco made Madrid
> the centre of everything, they'd have had to buy back
> the fish transported there and eat it looking out on the water
> they'd fished it from. They'd send their haul to Dublin now.

The seven short poems that make up 'The End of Goodbyes', reappear here to foreground Uncle James: 'He'd known too many people who/were looking well and they're all dead', he says of a man who emerges as another kind of doppleganger for his young nephew. And James brings a touch of romance; he still translated from Gaelic when he spoke, 'in tears with Mary, looking for a sign / his sister would remember she'd been here at all…' It was Mary's statement to the census man that resonated, cherished for the way it captured most schooling:

> "Qualifications?
> Mary said. "Put that we went to school
> and came home again all those years ago."

The sequence is a whistle-stop tour of people and places his mother needed persuading she knew, and there is great love for the people, though not for the institutions that would seek to control them. But for the fact we'd invented a make-believe tyranny where the word 'wonderful' was forbidden, especially when describing poems, I'd risk saying that the book is filled with a kind of wonder. Maybe nostalgia that gets into poetry springs from something we needed to leave behind. Or it could be the distance between bewilderment and rage is not so great.

An anthology of football poems would hardly burst its bindings, but *The Hungarian Who Beat Brazil* (2017) is surprising even for those who immediately know it refers to a football match. The setting is late 1950s and 60s, representing a troubled but hardly ruinous coming-of-age. Poems play out like documentaries, with an unscripted commentator musing as he goes along. The Hungarian is Florian Albert, who was at the heart of his country's 3-1 victory over the Brazilians in 1966. It is Albert who is admired by the speaker and his father, the latter saying 'He floated over grass / like a human hovercraft'. Albert's value lies in providing, 'the one thing we agreed on', which turns out to be artistry. Paul's dad is given to offer one of the most accurate descriptions the game has known. He finds his way into several other poems. In 'Sunday' the speaker recalls 'the month of them' it took him to 'cut your hair / the way you hate' while in 'Want' he talks of his dad's determination, in an Irish household, to make a better life for his children, even when the attempt led to his being 'banned from / many a house for keeping such stuff' from his kids – such stuff being the Irish question. We also see a Boston where no one appears to have heard of Robert Lowell. Even major figures get lost in cities that aren't seeking them. There's an abiding sense that Lowell, like Coltrane, never made it. The poet's apparent disappearance was more troubling to Paul than it looks, but there is no attempt to wring significance from these encounters. We're invited to smile ruefully rather than dial the psychiatrist.

Paul's search project in 2019 enabled a bringing-together of pairings and short sequences that would have been difficult or impossible in the chronological collections. The first half of these were published in *Whatever Else You Might Say* (2021) where two short poems called 'Gone' and 'Done' begin with son Thomas in a high chair forty years ago and end with Thomas and Sarah's daughter, Niamh. 'Gone' comes trailing religious undertones often parodied in earlier poems: 'your palms pushed out before you like the Pope'; the conclusion counterpoints the loss of a father with the birth of a son. The poem for Niamh begins in a kind of echo-chamber and goes on to refer to the great tidying itself, and the ways it, or we, might be considered 'done'. Childlike activity is echoed in what the adults have been doing, and a glance at the distinction between 'done' and the pain of parting is tinged with loss, even if a number of good poems had been uncovered in the purge.

The 'post-Hungarian' poems (2018-21) were never made

ready for publication but a sufficient number were indeed ready. 'The Chill Pill' begins a broad salvo against contemporary hates and 'What They Were Good At', written in 2020, looks into what some still call 'small wars'. I wondered where this idea was coming from before realising it was Auden (Paul was using old masters as spring-boards for new poems during lockdown).

Now, in March 2022, the uglier past is very much with us, and the poem looks eerily prescient. When the late Helen Dunmore wrote of Paul's ' rare clarity and exactitude' and Ann-Marie Fyfe expressed delight in his 'Irish exuberance for the absurd and the askew' they just about captured his full range between them. I recall someone saying that we admire Auden and love Eliot, but Paul would reverse the assertion. There's an immediacy, a clarity in Auden he was always striving for.

John Forth (March, 2022)

from

What Certainty is Like (1998)
What Moves Moves (2004)
Is This Like a Poem? (2022)
Forgetting to Come In (2007)

THE BRIDGE

Two boy-handle a canal gate's
wooden jib; one, his oilskin
brilliant yellow in the lashing rain,
transfers his weight by leaping
to his other foot;
the second, stiller, drab-green,
moves more deliberately,
as if he knows his craft.
They have no narrow boat,
no fishing rods,
they are playing with water,
with responsibilities, anticipating
slow rides everywhere.

A lorry sweeps across the water
gathering speed towards the motorway,
tyre-smooth, its hum mechanical,
its driver cursing his tachometer
and his luck. If he pushed it now
he'd reach the outskirts just
in time to beat the rush.
He presses on through rain
in shirtsleeves, braced against the spray.

AVANCEZ!

The Self-Service girl was not amused
by boys in Paris holding up her queue –
lunch was a busy time, we took too long.

Earlier we'd named the beauty by the pool
Annette because it began with A,
had fun dismissing all the Bs and Cs . . .

An hour meant nights in sharp-edged sheets,
my naked shoulders glistening like steak,
and not one of us spoke to a girl all week.

I tell all this, bringing you to the same hotel
and the same pool where you will turn
a golden brown and I'll be red again

though only enough to prove to you
how fast I burn. When the femme-de-chambre
clumsied-in and rolled-eyed out,

it was my groping for cover left me stranded.
You stretched one languid, backstroke
arm behind your head and smiled.

BEFORE THE MANAGERS CAME

Rats scurried along the lagging –
sometimes you'd find one cleaning the stockpot.
Hundreds, thousands of cockroaches collected
nightly under a table we'd have to lift and shake
over the stove until they'd all been burned.
Once when the Prince of Wales came late
we had to fish his *pommes parisienne*
out of the bin and he didn't notice and he didn't
complain. You never saw an inspector in the place
and you never heard of anyone poisoned either –

carcasses lay about ignored and someone
emptied the pig-bin once a week. Those were the days
we'd eat for next to nothing at home and drink
wine in half bottles and the occasional Volnay
smuggled out in a toc or the blue and white
check trousers we wore as chefs. The whole
building was blown up in the war, a direct hit,
while the customers danced in satin gowns.
It was the place to be seen in – and we bought the meat
and the vegetables and you ate real food.

MARKSBURG

The cannon trained
on the river's thoroughfare's
a joke cigar, its recoil
risking losses greater in
than out. I like to
make it fun by showing
the bed she slept in
sitting up (to keep her hair
in place) – the canopy
not for decoration
but for falling lice.

They used to crap here
through this hole,
fertilizing the garden below
where someone toiled
beyond the need for cures.

Climb the riders' staircase,
hire the dining hall,
see the pig's head choker
that weighed a grown
man down. Did you know
there once was an Iron-
Ox that roasted you alive?
That simple chain-mail
shirt you just ignored
cost twenty horses,
took the blacksmith
 years to make?

HOPE FOR HOUNSLOW

People believed the strangest things –
that a man climbed out of his grave,
that Job went on believing –
and they batter on the sides
of vans taking prisoners
to pre-trial hearings.

He'd heard the arguments
for God and lynch mobs,
first causes and inadequacies,
and knew only too well
that his speck of light
in time would be invisible.

He knew about mystery,
the strange unknowingness
of knowing – he believed in that.
Yet there were those who knew
for certain. How could you hammer
on the side of a van, or wave

a fist, or break into a sweat
of sin, unless you knew – or sing
outside the Holy Trinity Church
on Easter Saturday. He heard
their soulful harmonies before
he saw them lost in smiles

that had the ghostly spirit
in them. Something
welled up he wanted
to deny was sentiment.
Nor did he wish to take
a leaflet: *Hope for Hounslow.*

What he met there wasn't
integration but the uneasy
peace of those who hear
the angry rhetoric of black,
the angst of white, and cope.
There was a kind of hope in that.

If he could just survive the noise,
the waving and the arms raised
in salute, then so might God –
and he could handle that;
as he could marvel at the singers'
shy acceptance of applause.

THE MEN IN THEIR LIVES

1

She'd leave him to his football to read in bed
until she wondered what was keeping him
the night he gathered cushions, antimacassars
and anything else that came to hand into a neat
professional pile on the front room floor
and set light to it all.

All his life he'd laboured, digging, driving
caterpillars, tower-cranes, then staying behind
into his seventies to clear up after them,
to sweep the leavings of a day into a neat
professional pile on the floor of the yard
and set light to it all.

2

You wait to identify a body,
your father's. You know
he's dead, that he died

behind the wheel of the Rover
he'd picked up for a song,
but not that the car had slowed

almost to a standstill
on an almost imperceptible
incline while the lights

turned red, that dead
he'd veered gently
into an island bollard –

nor what you could expect
to be looking at, as if that
would make any difference.

3

Now my uncle's dead I'm back
watching an appalling mess of violet,
iterating dusty valedictions
and wondering at bewilderment
even years of Sundays can't suppress.

These are my family, none of them moneyed.
Every now and then I hear
my uncle's name inserted,
but it's no use. Funerals
make me think of me.

BOUTEILLE

Le Shuttle you'd have taken
in your stride, not knowing
what all the fuss was about,
or why it was needed.

   *

Turn off the D-road and you're there –
two houses lived in, a third for sale,
and a granary set aside like an empty carafe.

Bouteille – your daughter's *Quel trou!*
There are places like this back
in Ireland, but they don't have names.

And then it was Guilly and a signpost
for the Croix Tibi, a black memorial
in iron with its back to the Loire.

   *

So this is where you went to school,
and where you fished on holiday
not noticing the girls were bored

because kids being kids'll play anywhere;
where you walked away from Occupation,
all the way through France, over

the Pyrenees, and down
to Gibraltar's British Catering Corps;
where Nina's in beyond the mud

shallows, opening the urn,
tipping it under the breeze,
murmuring you've a lot to answer for.

*

René, some of you lodged in my eye!
But you'll be in heaven, you
were always sure of that

(for what had you ever done that was wrong?)
as if pride were the trick
invention of an educated fear.

And you went with the same
uncomplicated ease
that ruled your life, ill

for a couple of days, then dead,
the master chef who'd tell us
things are ready when they're done.

*

You're back in the Loire
at your own request –
and you've been through
a black hole under the sea
ferries criss-cross daily.

(i.m. René Metivier, 1911–1995)

TIME AND PLACE

His is no servant's voice, nor will his accent change
the further north we go: *"The buffet-car is open..."*

Then a flowering of vases stuffed with lids,
sandwich-cellophane and one-off spoons you can

blow bubbles through. The view is soporific, flat
until another row of spires I wouldn't notice

otherwise announces we're about to stop.
Valleys fall away along the local line;

chimneys pass through trees, attenuated towers
in a strange museum, or topless periscopes

whose dreadnaught mills rot in the undergrowth;
blackstone walls describe a helmet field, its visor

open on the hill, so perfectly the shape looks willed,
when yellow on a ground of green's what sets it off.

And there is distant conversation. What histories
have brought those two to lean against that fence?

Arriving is discovering namesakes everywhere
without my stir. Should I let the chalice pass,

I see their faces furrow, all conviction
melting on my tongue...

MARRY

Weddings have you noticing the backs of heads,
my father's for one, and, in the front pew,
Auntie Mary's, religious enough to be evil
we thought. Hers began increasingly to bob
involuntarily in a nervous tic, his to rock
to a private joke he couldn't quite control.
The bridegroom wasn't Irish
and hardly Catholic at all and she'd been
offering up novenas in the hope someone on high
would intercede to save her (and her daughter)
from intruders. "It's a thunderbolt
or nothing, now, my girl" he'd thought
as the vows approached and the backs of heads
told secrets you might miss head-on .

FATHER'S BROTHER, PADDY-JOE
(at The Blessed Oliver Plunkett Home, Dundalk)

The first time I saw him he was dead, a master cobbler
who'd served his time out lacing leather wallets sold in town
and improvising cushions visitors remarked on –
a private man, the sister told me, with a wicked, drunken tongue.

We cross the lawn in morning light, my father pocketing
the few particulars. A gardener lays aside his trowel
and stands to clasp his cap in a butterfly of hands
against his chest. We take a gravel path along the boundary wall

towards a brickshed mortuary. Inside the air is cold,
metallic, candles fizzing in it fitfully, like struck matches
left to burn, their light superfluous. There is incense
and the clink of thurible secreting charcoal clouds.

Continuously television carries pictures of the Pope
in Drogheda, where the Blessed Martyr's head's preserved,
a bullet-proof transporter nosing through the throng,
and helicopter shots of cars abandoned to their jams.

Next day, when we drive past, the roads are clear.
A wooden stage looks out on row after row of littered stalls
and a farmer, vexed, his faith examined by the mess
of yesterday, the thousands gathered for a miracle.

My mother's pleading with my father just to see the place.
He says there isn't time, his brother's dead, who wouldn't
have bothered his head about a Holy Father in a field.
He'd have kept himself to himself, as he usually did.

HOME
for my father

Halfway there,
the hearse broke down
irrevocably.

Our undertaker-driver
said it was lucky
he knew the local

man and all, who
dusted down an older
model, drove us on.

*

They're used to death
on Lissadell, were
sorry for our trouble;

they had dug the grave.
My hand slipped
shovelling earth

onto the coffin's
velvet cushion –
stone on wood's

too cold to contemplate.
*I'd stick to the pen
if I were you,*

the old priest said.
It pleased him,
my ineptitude.

*

In Ellen's ancient bar,
Michael tots up
drinks in pencil.

I'm introduced to Pat,
who's had an education,
says the English

knew they'd win
destroying the Irish tongue.
Few speak it here.

Dun an doras isn't   (Shut the door)
much to know,
or *dun do bheal*   (shut your mouth)

   *

You're with the men
you went to school with
fifty years ago, asking

what they know about Micky
Flynn. Who'd have thought it
of cousin Ellie, a bastard son?

   *

We found the undertaker
in his grocer's shop.
He couldn't live by death alone.

*Sure, you'll be over
soon enough again,
why don't you pay me then?*

   *

How could he know
you have no reason
to return, that she

had been the last of us?
Even the field you
thought was yours

has gone to Micky
in the States. All
that's left for you

to smile about is Pat
traipsing back from
Ellen's in the afternoon

to see us off, his cows
waiting in the lane
to lead him home.

NICKING THE CHURCH LEAD

Abroad for the first time with Mr Lloyd
a small boy notices on Sunday
that the priest is saying early mass alone.
He thinks about it and seeing a chance
to be both helpful and heroic decides
that, yes, he will take the place
of the absent altar boy – which he does
by walking up the centre aisle,
opening a gate in the communion rail
then closing it silently behind him.
He knows the Latin by heart and kneels
appropriately on the bottom step.
The priest acknowledges him discreetly,
almost imperceptibly, leaving him vaguely
disappointed, and continues unperturbed.

*

What brought it back was meeting Mr Lloyd again –
calling him "Sir" outside an examination room
and hearing him whisper "Call me Dick" –
waiting in the street for our appointed time,
would-be Masters of Education sharing a joke
about the places literature and theology meet.
When I visited him in his primary school (ours
had been only the second class he'd taught)
he asked about my secondary years. He was afraid
a number of boys had lost their faith around that time.
Jones, Campbell, Rostron, Bond had all gone on
to the seminary and they'd all returned.

My mother still has the letter I wrote
from Blankenberge. When I gave it to him to post
Dick Lloyd had smiled about the handwriting
which was his – or at least my version of it.
When people comment on my writing now

I tell them everyone does something well.

*

Why was it when Fr Halvey arrived
I'd have one foot on a straight-backed chair
and the other in the sink to wash my knees?
His tetchiness was legendary, the result
of something more than *what-if* questions
from a boy. He'd sprinkle cruet water
at ablutions in your face and make you
make mistakes. Priests were not to be spoken to
let alone argued with but he wanted me
to study for the priesthood. I said no.
I did feel holy once, going to Benediction
when it wasn't even my turn to serve –
but it didn't last. The twentieth century
may be engaged in a doomed experiment
to live without God but I tell you,
in our house, if you didn't experiment
you lost your way. It's sad a glass of Dick Lloyd's
sherry's not enough to bridge the gap.
One's in Australia; Tony Jones came back
and went to jail for nicking the church lead.
God knows what happened to the rest.

ANOTHER BREAK-IN

Your jewellery was the first and worst of it.
Since then it's been the video each time
and not much else. This latest haul comprised
a bottle of Moet and a dictaphone,
our son's Nintendo with accessories
and games, and the envelope you left
leaning against a vase to give your mum
on Sunday when she came. There was
money in the vase, but not the card.

It's not so much that one becomes inured
as thankful burglars round these parts
are not too bright. My post-war Selmer S.A.
would bring in more than all they'd nicked
but it was in its case beside soprano, flute
and clarinet – and the Nintendo doesn't work.
The police were stretched and way behind,
came hours late. P.C.Bradley asked
the usual questions and informed us

someone from Serious Crime would be
in touch, it was amazing now the effect
of DNA, you sometimes catch them
five years on, when they've been collared
for another job. He'd be after blood
and shiny surfaces, you never know,
but with two of them to cover all
the crime, if a murder should come in,
well, we would have to wait our turn.

It's what they *didn't* take, we said. He put
his notebook down and beamed, had been
in brass bands all his life and the Vincent
Bach trumpet, euphonium and old French Horn
had all survived when he'd been done.
My Super Action had him drooling like a kid.

And it could have been anything up to
half an hour before he was back to wonder
had he left his torch behind. He had.

WHATEVER MICK WANTS
for Michael McLoughlin

If you were ever vexed or moved
you left no clues. They could
have put a gun to your head
and you wouldn't have flinched.

You turned without a word and left
that time the barman pointed to a notice
about the need to dress 'refined'.

Your best friend stalked his future wife
with year-long valentines. You scaled
your girlfriend's drainpipe
in the jacket riddled with bullet-holes
the barman banned.

Your tenor sax speaks jazz with the same
lazy filling up of space
you lead everyone to think you'll leave unfilled.

STORY

The yard I can tell you about
with its well and stone, and the walls
veined and resolute against the heat.
The camps were open secrets
yet we slept – I'm sure living
on the faultline hardened us,
but not to unconcern. Our solitude
was jealous, something shared.

The night they shot and drowned
my husband, crushed my son's skull
with rifle butts and searched the house,
I was hiding in a cupboard, struggling
to stifle my daughter's screams.
When I let her go I'd smothered her.

They say I'm cold because I married
again – but he helped me back when I
could think of nothing but that night,
until I loved him – and I love him still.
I don't need telling that he's one of *them*
but he was there, on no one's side

but mine. Oh, I can see how useful
I am now to both their causes,
but I cannot stomach all this talk
about our comfortable peace. If I
spoil their story, they will write it anyway,
so let them write it any way they will.

ANYWAY AND ANYWAY

When she was sawn in half she could choose
the roads not taken, try out husbands, lovers,
like goods on approval, without their knowing;
she could join another act and choose to dispense
with the man on the ground to break her fall
by landing somewhere else, leaving him
waiting, clutching at nothing at all
while his eyes took fright; she could buy
not necessarily expensive frocks to see
what they made of her, the children behaving
or not behaving, and no one would know.

It wasn't because her life intact was bad.
It was just a mess of probabilities,
when what she wanted once in a while
was what she'd heard called a futurable,
though she couldn't find one, even in books.

Over and over she emerged from her partner's
box of partitions to bright lights and applause
as thunderous as dwindling audiences allowed,
until she hardened to a thirty-something
of exquisite delicacy aficionados wanted
to rescue from one-night galleries and put on show
in their homes, though they worried over its
authenticity – sometimes she'd pretend
in a range of voices as if she'd out-Seller
Sellers if she could, the boys loving it,
the grown-ups never sure – until
she hardened into something beautiful
that might have been a chatelaine
adored by servants in another life.

SANARY-SUR-MER

She climbs out of her shift and pays
ten francs for a lilo to the beach-boss
who has rushed his torso and his
squeaky voice across to share a joke.

She adjusts the ivory teeth about her neck,
ties her hair back, lets her breasts subside
and slides slowly down until her legs
are gentled firmly to a fearless V.

Muscularities are at her feet
like moths for volleyball
but get no closer than retrieving
ricochets, are left to play for real.

The man who picks her up at five
must be her husband, and
the mini-belle their daughter.
She's serene enough. I don't watch

all of this each time, of course –
sometimes she's lying there when I arrive.
It's possible that somewhere else
you've heard about my ritual from her.

THE ACT OF UNIFORMITY

1

Before next Yuletide, a fearful pestilence
will lay waste the land and myriad souls
be loosened from their flesh and the valley
will be full. Said Dorothy Dinglet's ghost.

It was either that or divine retribution
visited on a village that allowed its kids
to drive a young cow into the church
and giggle when it fouled the nave.

2

William Boghurst, the apothecary, laid
a Puppy Dog upon his patient's breasts
and made her drink Dill, Pennyroyal, Fennell,
Aniseed Water for two or three hours together,
for she was a fat woman and could bear it.
Others set the plucked tails of pigeons
to their sores for as long as the pigeons died.

3

What feat of oratory, of argument, kept them there?
Was it made easier by those who tried to get away,
the woman stoned at Tideswell who returned?
Mompesson couldn't have managed it alone.
And nor could Stanley. These were troubled times,
the church and a republican in league.

4

How firm their faith! No more funerals
or churchyard burials – they say none were
interred before they'd breathed their last –
and services to switch to Cucklet Dell
out in the open air. They called the hill
Golgotha. Katherine Mompesson,
though rambling towards the end,
answered William's religious questions
from the Book of Common Prayer
as if in perfect health. He was consoled
that God should be so gracious to her
in her time of need. 'Ah, Mompesson,
the air! How sweet it smells!'

FOUR WAYS OF LOOKING AT A CABINET

The sales pitch for kit was a glass-fronted cabinet
in the entrance hall, beside the cups and shields
that spelled a kind of history of the place.

Now, the cabinet is history stuck in the assembly hall
until another use be found for it. A blue-tacked
strip says *S c h o o l E n t e r p r i s e s*.

As if the days of capital were gone, the upper
shelf has slipped from hooped supports and hangs,
its sugar-paper coating ripped and snagged.

The War Memorial's behind the cabinet.
*Their name shall remain forever and their glory
shall not be blotted out* is blotted out.

THE BICYCLE GARDEN

The graves of children who go missing
are abandoned bicycles set in concrete
bases lowered into shallow trenches
by the railway bridge and left to rust.
The engineer (retired) who tends
the place says visitors are few –
he imagines parents driving slowly by
or peering through the wire-mesh fence
for a particular shade of paint or rake
of handlebar, but they don't come in.

And there it was, this gaunt tableau
of BMXs, racers, mountain bikes,
an aged Vespa with its fairing crushed,
and tricycles with tassels tied to handlegrips
or crossbars, where they stayed, seeming,
to those who looked, to rise up from the ground
or sink into it. You turn away –

because there's no such garden, though
the bicycles are often all that's found.
An end-page columnist invented it,
when it seemed to him society
was waging war on being young,
on children who enticed and let you
down. So he dreamed a garden for them,
and the engineer was somehow odd
enough to make the whole thing real,
a sleight that left its maker lying
with the silence in his ears, as if
some violence had been done.

CHRISTINA'S WORLD

There are no lorries drowning out
the opening of *Music for Strings, Percussion and Celeste*,
the floor juddering and you so used to it
you hardly notice. There is no arterial road,
just a single track of wheel-ruts,
curving in parallel, like the first impression in snow.
It fades over the hill and out of sight,
and might be endless.

Was any of this here yesterday? A single house,
a roof-high ladder circumflexed in front.
There are outhouses, a lean-to, and a barn
set half a distance back. This is the beginning
of suburbia, and when the word gets round,
it will become the town. Christina wakes,
levers herself up from grass, and turns to look
back towards a house that will be streets away.
Wyeth watches from an upper room and paints
her world. She drags herself into a locust-crawl.
The cart will turn to truckers' rigs, ladder to cranes
that fill out city skyscapes, sway above a maze
of messages, anticipating more.

HAND-ME-UPS

These days I've taken to wearing my son's cast-offs, stuff
that looks nearly new to me: a cream jumper with graded
hoops of blue, my first leather jacket and a clutch
of shirts, including a fake Lauren, the horse and rider
sewn on too near the button-fly. He'd never wear the thing.

Another bears a tag, says Martinique, though whether
that's both company and place, I wouldn't know.
I do know that it's classier than anything I own,
have to acknowledge that it's better made, of better
quality. Not Jermyn Street, but better than I've got.

So, new is where it's at, and it surprises me to learn
I look OK. I cannot be the first to be allowed to slip into
what strikes me as a novel category – not the well-worn
hardy stuff inherited from a brother, older and into
more fashionable gear that fits. I'm limited,

of course, to what fits me, my broad shoulders,
and my being inches taller, but I'm grateful for
what comes my way. He smiles, showing Dad
that, after all, there's something in the style
that's been beneath him all these years.

PRESSING

In every room a hyphened-alphabet moons down
like logos wedged on driving-school cars;
so many records JAZZ alone might fill
a concert hall. And there are corridors off
to search for what is missing, temporarily –
a place so cavernous you cannot browse.

Cologne had earlier disturbed you into silence,
all of a sudden switching lanes and gripping
the wheel harder on your one way through.
Then, as suddenly, you relaxed into a summary
of diplomatic number plates, your own
a very minor grade, far from immune.

And what an orgy of packaged art to preface
our return to Bonn, its modern embassies,
your English school; Le Carre country's
foreign field where Roger (who you know's a spy)
wears street-wise polaroids and Bogart macs
an incident could ruffle, pack off home.

Scotch slips down with Hubbard's fluegelhorn
and fades-in memories of draughty nights
in transit-vans outside the likes of Swansea.
The other side starts playing circus music
by a military band, but even Cologne
by now's too far, too far to take it back.

SKY WOMAN IN NEW YORK

In the mythology of the Iroquois and Huron, the Woman Who Fell From the Sky is a primal ancestor. Also known as Sky Woman or Ataensic, she plays a central role in creation.

Here you buy fags at the pharmacy
but can smoke them only at a single table
by the bar with a ceiling fan directed at you.
Or not at all. Last night it was not at all.
You were forced into the street after the veal
cursing the world and its crusades.

When Sky Woman fell through the hole
grabbing at the roots of the uprooted
Celestial Tree, she brought gifts
of tobacco and the wild strawberry
to earth. Tobacco grew from her daughter's
chest and wild strawberries at her feet.

None of this cuts any ice. With the strawberry
tamed, and smoking all but banned,
eating out's increasingly a matter of *on bouffe
et on part*, which is no longer rude.
When ordering a second bottle of wine
alarms adjoining tables and transports

the restaurateur to a delirium of smiles,
what is there left to do but eat and go?
The argument is lost, at least for now –
even Sky Woman would protest She
wasn't to know (if, privately, convinced
some kinds of regulation can be dull).

AMONG THE DOUBLEGANGERS

I've often been mistaken for Ken Smith
and if you could see my photo you'd know
how a friend of twenty years standing
could make a beeline for Ken Smith
thinking he was me though I've never turned
my back and read my poems to the wall.
In fact, I'm one of the nicest poets
I'm ever likely to meet, though I'm told
I need to work on the razzled look.

At the library a talking lift exhaled
a breath of librarians, and the man waiting
to greet them claimed he was me
which (swap an *a* for an *o*, I said) he was
but he was far too busy to smile.

Even the book I'd borrowed had been recalled
by a Paul McLoughlin, though whether
or not there's a third of me is unresolved.
I'm thinking of writing to Paul 2 & 3
and Ken to warn them we're becoming
an old joke. You must know the one:
someone looks at a full-frontal Smith and says
I don't know who he is, but isn't that
McLoughlin standing next to him?

THE GREY DOG OF SWORDLAND

They'd kick me out just now for what I did,
but I'd try anything to motivate the boys –
I bought a goat for one to tend; another two
I set to building a wall we didn't need.
It taught them measurement, and baffled
the inspector who couldn't put his finger on
quite what he knew was wrong.

The dog appeared when we were camping
near Morar. The locals were resigned
and sure enough we heard within a month
of a clansman's death. I have to admit
it rattled me, but back at school I had to quell
a bout of boys absconding – they were always
caught, but always with a string of crimes:

a dozen break-ins, seventeen stolen cars –
so I made up Mary of the Turret, a tormented soul
who'd fallen to her death next door, and had
a colleague don a sheet and strap a torch inside.
Once they'd seen her in the dead of night,
they all stayed put. For days I watched them
checking they were all of them alive.

WHISTLING

There's a man down at the Treaty Centre,
whistling, one foot a way in front of
the other and he's rocking to and fro,
whistling, his long, white-tipped stick
stretching into a deep and lidless
tub where coins are rising.

Lately, we've been spoilt –
Peruvian pipes; a jack-in-the-box
of a singer of jaunty songs, who skips
round little children, makes them laugh;
a pensioner in a straight-backed chair
crooning into a mike to pre-recorded
tapes, Jim Reeves smoochy style;
even a blind accordionist whose playing
is an undifferentiated wash of sound.

But today none of these regulars,
just the whistler with the precinct
to himself. He takes a break, enjoys
a laughing conversation with a
punter or a passer-by. And still he rocks,
forward and back, forward and back,
his eyes enough to tell us he is blind.

But whistling? The tunnel of shops
behind him is filling up with fellow
whistlers joining in – the melodies
old familiars: *Bright Eyes, Somewhere
Over the Rainbow*, and *Alone Again,
Naturally*. He isn't the greatest
whistler, the high notes clipped
as if they might be missed, but
we'll get used to him, come to accept
that we've been entertained.

KNOW WHAT I MEAN?
for John Forth

We've known since Copernicus
the sun never sets, yet selenologists
feed us photos of the earth
rising, as if our moon's the new
still centre of a universe
that might, for all I know,
be shifting.
              I'm no scientist
and I'm not averse to metaphor,
but what moves moves.

You'll say it doesn't matter
much, that Earthset times
would cause no panic
of near-misses in the sky
nor would the hours of daylight
change.
       But
misinterpretation has a history
of repeating itself. Does
every near-miss mean
someone intended to collide?

THAT WAS A WAY OF PUTTING IT

Between the whistle which you did not hear
and the whistle which you will not hear
there are corners, a time for repossession.
Not turning points for there is no turning
but moments when the ball is still.

Odd moments you may try to prepare for
when the ball is still but all else is movement;
a time to escape from the shady defender,
a chance to rise to the chance appearance
when manoeuvres suggest that the chances are few;

when success only means you return to the centre
for the game is not over, just older,
and the final score will not disclose
if the goal for or the goal conceded
came at thirty minutes or eighty-nine.

WHAT CERTAINTY IS LIKE

The jib had idled back above the half-built block
so when, not knowing this and unconcerned till then
at playing clothes' peg to a monstrous line,
he fell, the concrete caught him far too soon.

But not before he'd lived his life again – you
wouldn't believe how long it takes to plummet
fifteen feet. Knowing what *might* happen,
it's tough imagining what certainty is like.

Second-guessing's second nature most of the time.
Don't tell Mum or Dad the bump on your head's
some nutter not a door – they'll only ground you
saying you should be in before pubs turn out.

Why risk tanked-up rough-houses asking
what your problem is when you can give nothing
a chance to happen and then have all night
to set about them in the dark.

AT THE WATERMANS

1. Little Voice

Come Fly With Me. We should have known
this would be about homing pigeons
and human birds in search of flight,
a little voice that's silent when it's not
impersonating Garland, Monroe, Bassey

for the Dad who's dead, and Telephone Bill,
the heartthrob at her window, not on a ladder
but hoisted on a cherry-picker cantilevered
to his BT van. His precious Dwayne flies home
from Europe as we knew it would, but lands

on her window ledge, not his. We're watching
cinema's equivalent to all those first flutterings
in verse, children writing peoms about brids,
the spelling mistakes a kind of stumbling
into speech. She helps him exercise the birds.

2. 'Round Midnight

Dexter Gordon's playing someone much like Dexter Gordon
thawing out in Paris, his *machinery* obsessed with saving
Gordon's sound and, with it, him. Europe loves its New York
legends, though they still play small on West Third Street.

A rock star said when Coltrane died it was a shame
he never made it. There's a clean-cut trio steaming in the bar
when we come out, and a jazz-freak in the foyer selling Monk.

3. Il Postino

You can book if you like, but Tuesday afternoon
for an Italian film with English subtitles
and a Chilean poet? There'll be no one there.

The place was packed. Latecomers were forced
apart by an old-age pilgrimage alive
to weekday rates – and no one made a sound.

This was new, an older generation better
educated than the young, better able
to look out for itself and, for all we knew, surprised

the local bookseller was not on hand
with a job lot of Neruda
specially bought in.

FRAGMENTS OF HUMANITY
On a woodcut by Hans Holbein

A cadaverous timpanist is stirring
thickly in a brace of deep tureens
soup that would sustain him were it soup.

He's hammering skins with gusto
in an orchestra of bones. Brass is hauled
somehow to the horizontal, breathed into life.

Skulls crowd the square to celebrate
the possibility of air. One weighed down
with keyboard and the mallet that's clipped on

is wearing shades under a ringlet wig; another's
resting humerus on knee to smoke a horn.
There are occasional hats and limp intestines.

They're playing for all they're worth.
When they disperse, disintegrate,
charitable fumigators will move in.

CHILDREN OF THE SUN

Granting these people places on
our course is reckless of
the fuss they make of words.
Agreed, it isn't wise to turn down
anyone with a degree
of aptitude and I admit they can
write, but poets have no
stomach for the elasticity of
truth we're looking for. Bonking
celebs a pair of compasses?
This kind of stuff won't wash,
and no self-respecting writer'd
get out of bed for what a poet
calls an audience. We're talking
breakfast tables here and over-
crowded tubes and comfort breaks,
so I say train 'em up and put 'em
on the Subs' bench – the soft sods
are, I'm told, reliably grammatical,
and some can spell, and punning
headlines might be up their street.

PHILISTINE

For every thousand people there's nine hundred doing the work, ninety doing well, nine doing good, and one lucky bastard who's the artist...
– (Henry Carr in Tom Stoppard's *Travesties*)

I know it's a soft drainpipe,

but it could equally well be flabby
cock and balls, or elephant's trunk and ears –
a tease (pulley-adjustable) of curtain material.

My kind of cloth – I know
what to do with it, how to measure it,
cut it, line it, allow it to drop before stitching
the hem. I could twist it, ruche it,
let someone write about it.

I also know about the orange
that's not an orange because
it's a painting of an orange,
a brilliant orange and huge, you want
to squeeze out the juice and drink it.

A room under repair exhibits an
arrangement of paint-pots, plastic
sheeting and a pair of leaning tyres.
'Untitled' and a gloss would point out
what I need to bring to it.

As for the hanging whatever-it-is,
were I to withdraw its explanation,
unclasp its tie-back, and fit
a window in the wall behind it,
we should see St. Paul's.

GROUCH
for Brian Jones

You once said that where we end up
is a pretty good indication of where
we were always going. By then
we've wasted time not recognising
who we are, or hoping it might be
otherwise, our pillowed heads
resisting what's insidiously true.

Someone I wouldn't give a letter to post
(and I was right), I later learned
I'd met with a grunt. My father
grunted, and I've been fighting him off
ever since – something I choose
to do, because I tell myself I can.

Otherwise who cares, If we stick around
long enough we'll only turn into
the selves who stuck around, and few
would welcome being young again
without knowing what they know,
or knowing it, if that means knowing
where they're going is where they are.

CHANNEL HOPPING

1

Here is a time for wanting
to write without irony,
to eliminate the wry
distance of humour, to let
the serious have its say,
free from the cushioned landing
that turns grimace into smile.

It's not as if the witty's
trivial, its rather that
sometimes it seems a cheap way
out of facing up to life,
to squalor, sleaze and slaughter,
celebrity and clamour,
and the Sunday magazines.

2

Keeping catch isn't easy
for grizzly Alaskan bears
in summer. A single bear
can eat three-plus kilos worth
of salmon up in numbers
for a once-in-a-lifetime
chance to reproduce themselves,

but there are far too many
other bears, none of whom must
relish the congestion, or
stealing from another mouth –
but this is the way things are,
join in or starve. We're wary
of bears lest they do us harm.

3

"What's the news from the White House,
Mark?" "Well, Anna, I'm afraid . . ."
Jesus! Is this some kind of
transcontinental garden
gate, a private audience?
Are we supposed to be here
listening? Should we go away

and let these people get on
with their sparkling other lives?
Their entitlement to fame?
Flamingos queue politely
for water safer than the
toxic, equatorial
stuff they find their algae in.

4

Olga who thinks she's human
is looking now for more than
a lap to lie in. Something's
wrong. It isn't rational
to suppose she's playing on
our sympathy. She's in pain.
It is no laughing matter,

nothing artful remedies
might cure, even if laughter
means we're a cut above bears.
She knows nothing about queues,
would freeze in Alaska, flee
from bigger bears. Perhaps there's
something in us she can see.

BIRDS

For me, it's never been the violence of size,
of eagles, or vultures, or crows, that petrifies

but the smaller species whirring invisible
electrical saws, mad flutterings, unable

to escape. A robin in a room's bad enough
if it's in a flap, but aviaries are the stuff

of nightmare. Dozens of the frantic things.
The thought of being in there, frozen trembling,

the glass they might fly headlong into!
I'd feel invisible and spare. I know I'm meant to

be beyond all this – I should be able to list
them, know their names, and could, if you insist,

consult the latest Field Guide, but I'd be lying
telling more than is the case – which is: it's flying,

the movement of wings, that makes me turn away
in terror (*They won't come, will they?*), and pray

they'll be kept in check. Hendren just freaked
when rehearsed in a cage of black-beaked

villains. I'm not surprised ornithophobia
set in. Mine's less clear: a rootless fear,

my mother thought, though Mr. Freud'd
say that simply telling the unembroidered

truth was going to be cure enough, or else
in the end it's sex like everything else.

FLUGEL
for Dick Pearce

What happened to the flugelhorn
you always played, that had you
turn down trumpet gigs, the famous
brother too brash, too much
like the army that could not
sustain itself on minor modal scales?

Did you buy yourself out, grow
your hair, practise, practise, find
the melting, mellow sound of
private life less trumpet loud, play
the fatter horn, because it caught
a quieter, self-effacing mood?

You were never one for soaring
high, preferring Miles to Dizzy
any day, Rollins to Bird. Is it
because bewildered in a world
you can't believe you helped create,
you must speak louder now?

So many lack technique, can only
marvel at a winged horn that puffs
the air with proof that gentle rain
can slake a giant thirst. Did it grow
too comfortable, so much the salve
you locked away its charm for good?

As if suddenly you were a sophist
duping those who'll follow any lure
that takes them out beyond the boom
of modern gods towards the human
birdsong that's heartsease if only
temporarily, then temporarily at least.

ON MAGRITTE'S 'MAN OF THE SEA' (1926)
For the student of Literature who asked which bits of David Copperfield *he should read.*

I'm a diver in black with bulges in all the right places
except where it matters. My head is musical, a pre-shaped

violin. I am obsessed with bits of wood, cross sections
of latticed table, painters' palettes, and the jigsaw cut-outs

I stand on to lever open a plane door to a paler sky
that has ignored its meeting with the sea. A stone corner-piece

suggests the fireplace complete. It's all we need. The gist.
Why waste time on the whole affair. We know the stories

of table, fireplace, floor, hear the music of sea and sky
from a bar or two. I read only dust-jackets, consult synopses

in my guide to films. You'll say no one can tell the final score
five minutes into a match, and I'll concede it's sometimes true,

but not nearly often enough to warrant ninety minutes,
extra time, or five days in extremis for a draw. Get it

over with. Move on. Nothing's worth the time it takes.
I don't need ears or nose or mouth. I know a block

of solid sand shifts somewhere beneath my feet, that it will
crack like ice and in my element there'll be no more of me.

GOING

There is apparently significance
in numbers. Thirty years
is a carriage clock. There are those

who ensure they're never seen
again where they've been paid to be,
who start up other lives,

but the end of things is nothing
else to go to beyond whatever
is believed, and is the case

for all of us, members of one club
or another whether we choose
to join or not. Or leave.

The good in us will always
forget. It's nothing
rotten in our state. It's just

the way we are, and clocks
ignore us everywhere we look,
or cry, or celebrate, or think

somehow we could have
made things right. Some people
have the carriage clock

some time before they leave,
before they know that going
is arriving somewhere else.

THERE'S ALWAYS THIS

She is wearing money and straight black hair,
and, standing close, looks up at him, is kissed,
a million miles away from mortgages
and kids, though not, perhaps, from paying cash
and nannies. On a Metro station, they
believe in love, for it's themselves they love
for capturing each other. Suddenly,
there are people on platforms everywhere
I look, kissing, and on Eurostar where
a high-heeled blonde won't leave her stubbled beau
alone for long, will thread a bangled arm
around his neck and bare her perfect teeth.
Speed turns up the volume on the outside
world, and snow is angling to come in.

THE GOOD CATHOLIC

Miss Robinson ruled her Tea Rooms like a headmistress
in a black dress down to her ankles, her pet monkey,
chained to the door of the oven range, grabbing coins
from customers and storing them in its bulging jaws.

I'd half-a-crown, a fortune that I showed and lost
and slapped the creature good and soundly, hoping
I'd be linked by no one to its piercing scream.
I boasted it remembered me. I wanted to be free.

Next door in the picture theatre, the blessed monkey
will not let me be. It revels in its right to misbehave.
By the time Messala bites the dust, I've had enough
of Judah Ben-Hur and being good. I want it dead.

MARGARET BY THE FIRE

Mum had taken her in for her to sit on the rug
in front of the fire doing nothing. I listened to her

being talked about, how she wasn't moving
a muscle to find a job. I got into trouble once

for saying as much to her face. She was like
a whey-faced pet, had something to do

with Mickey, a good-for-nothing weasel
of a man Dad said was nothing more

than she deserved. She'll be dead by now
but resurrects herself. I'd read Mickey's

athletics' programmes while the adults talked
of stuff I hadn't a clue about, like de Valera.

He was not to be confused with Mick,
the man we reached through hushed corridors

in Hammersmith. I was made to sit
in an anteroom with nothing to do

but marvel at a height of ceiling
and the weight of wood in the doors.

When Dad came out, we hurried home,
his turn-ups flapping against his ankles.

This Mick was clearly not the sort of man
who'd want to be dealing with Margaret.

FIRST FLIGHT
for Colin & Diana Miller

Every generation discovers ice, Icarus falling
from a marble sky he thought himself attached to,
that fire burns no matter who your dad is,
and that breathing-in the triumph is a cut above
the fancy dress of taking everyone's advice.
Bronze is heavier than air, and more expensive.
Survival's shortfall comes with learning
someone got there first, that every muscle's
been stretched as far as it'll bear before, that better
toning's led to faster times and longer lives.
Flying's humdrum nowadays, a kind of ice,
as if falling's failure were a form of hope,
and falling now took longer than it did.

from *The Road to Murreigh* (2010)

FIRSTLINGS
Murreigh, 1952

My brother, strapped to his high-chair and not yet two,
    left so much milk and glass on the stone floor
I was forever back and forth to Hannah's where I'd watch her
    rummage, smiling, through the bottles she'd put by
for yet another that would take the teat.

I was five. Now you tell me you were pregnant again,
    that when the men stopped off at Begley's
for a drink, and stayed, you made your own way
    to the ceilidh on the strand, and couldn't see
the harm in dancing with the local garda till they came.

They never came. The next day you miscarried,
    nearly died, the same Hannah whispering
in your ear about the poor policeman waiting for you still
    at the water's edge. You'd no sympathy –
he'd two eyes in his head to see your wedding ring.

I must have noticed you were gone for days, but I only see
    the bottles fall and hear myself complain
about the floor. *Boyeen,* my uncle said, *if ever you're over here*
    to see us again, we'll put a car pet down,
and have it stretching out from here across the water.

HAVING THE GIFT

It's a long way to Holyhead by night,
then to arrive as close to America as Ireland gets,
to see the very picture I'd imagined in the train's
dark window: a whitewashed cottage with its whitewashed
garden wall. There was a gate you had to drag
off the ground, and a forge I'd stand outside
at one end of a path that petered out to grass –
and nettles I'd fall in though I'd been forever warned.

If the cottage came while I was travelling backwards
all those years ago through Wales, I couldn't see
the peat fields the men set off for every morning
with the horse and cart. Once they did say yes, laughing,
only to put me down in the lane. They wouldn't be
keeping a constant eye on me, for fear I'd disappear.

THE NOISE

Names disappear and the door is closed now to
cups of tea and the time of day, and we'll all be tourists
soon. It's a terrible thing you can't eat this landscape.

He went for lobsters years ago in Baile na nGall
but it was murderous work and there was no money in it
at ten shillings a dozen with the lobsters rare.

They rarely venture out along the stream he'd fix
a path of stones across only for the children to come
laughing and move them so what was the point.

Mostly it rains but now, just now, the Atlantic's
so calm you'd hardly know it was there. Shadows
patch the hills and drift and it's light till ten, a slow smile

waiting for the frown to descend through mist over Brandon –
but it's better than the noise when he was in Chicago
where you cannot sleep. O, it's better than the noise.

MOTHER IN MURREIGH

You wanted to be seventy
here – despite your brother
being the most contrary man
ever to put shoes on his two feet.

You spent the morning up at Peggy
Hanafin's exchanging litanies
of the dead with friends
you hadn't seen for thirty years.

How may the old ways endure
with the children elsewhere
and not a word to be said
for the one or two who stayed?

I watch you blow out the candles
on your cake, and think of Mary
over yonder, who was dead for days
before they picked her off the stone floor.

For the umpteenth time you ask
contrary James how many
sugars has he in his tea. The smile
he shakes his head with's meant for me.

A LITTLE TREAT FOR JAMES

It started in a Scandinavian-style café
looking out on the bay. I filched
a sheet of paper (I always have a pen)
and with the help of another (strong)
coffee a poem appeared: *Names
disappear and the door is closed now
to cups of tea and the time of day ...*

The yard across from St Mary's
saw me come and go, organize
a birthday cake for mum this afternoon,
buy a pad of cartridge paper,
(not too dear) then copy out the poem
(a large-tipped felt-tip thing)
and get it mounted in a scarlet frame.
An adventure for a cloudy day
unfolding in an art-shop and a baker's,
the unusual to everyone's delight.

And James was chuffed and had me
read it out. Mum said the cake was nice,
the kind she used to make, but why
did I have to say the door was closed.
James hid the poem in a drawer.
I doubt it saw the light of day again.

FISHING RIGHTS

Community means Europe trawling Norse-named shores
    with Gaelic caught in the Gaeltacht if at all.
    Smerwick gulls, like cats-eyes, stand in shallow water
and house-ends are sails across the bay above the one-field farms
that can't afford farmers living the life of Reilly as they do.

Armada Spanish hid in these hills and changed their names.
    Had they stayed at home till Franco made Madrid
    the centre of everything, they'd have had to buy back
the fish transported there and eat it looking out on the water
they'd fished it from. They'd send their haul to Dublin now.

Like your man Joe who'd always complain, arriving late
    to set up his stall in Maine Street, that the Upper
    you go the Mainer they get. But they've gone,
to England or the U.S.A., leaving a lobster pot
to lie on its side in the sand like a sweepstake tumbler.

A row-boat's chained in rust to a concrete disc beside
    a spreader that made whirling tracks around it
    in the early hours, an empty plaything with a cone.
If there's little left to fertilise anyway here, at least
    the lichens' green is green – and it's colour,

    fresh as the breeze you huddle from, you notice most,
and the gulls, and how far back where you come from goes.

MAIRE DE BARRA
for Marian

Knowing how to enter a pub, your man
follows in behind his faithful pianist,
doffs his hat to the cheers he's greeted with,
and throws his arms high and wide, forgetting
it was Good Friday only yesterday.

An American tells me I'm a dead ringer
for Kurt Vonnegut Jnr., and I joke
he'll have me talking backwards next
about the war; which isn't our favourite
bit—we can't remember the book it's in,
but there are two characters and the man
orders a drink only for Vonnegut to
remind us he can make the girl drink
anything he likes—which, of course, she does.

Someone's sidled in who wouldn't know
if anyone looked like a writer
but it doesn't surprise him when a young
blackguard's rude to the landlord
because we all know being hit when we were
young did nobody any harm. Now, he says,
you can't even use language on them,
the kids who don't know how to go on.

And suddenly I'm back in Murphy's eating
a Beef-and-Guinness pie with the BSE war
still raging, overhearing a blonde one going
on at her fella because he hadn't given her
a bite of his burger when she'd asked,
and it was no use offering her a whole one
now, because the damage was done
and if she was bothering him she couldn't
care less, she didn't want him breathing
in her fucking face.

The Hat is into his act by now with *Elvisis-
Alive-and-Well-and-Living-Here-in-Dingle*,
rhyming Rasta with faster once young Malcolm
from Jamaica's gone. And his eyes alight
on Mum and he knows she's a gift from heaven
at seventy-six and he works on her all night
until she's out on the floor dancing with him,
telling him her children haven't a step in their leg,
and claiming she's never been so embarrassed
in all her life, with the pianist insouciant
as if there's nothing he doesn't know.

The Hat is hoping we didn't mind and we say
it's unlikely she'll remember any of this
– it's why we're here, her last trip home;
and isn't it something being proposed to,
even in jest, and being applauded from the floor.

So here I am talking to Kurt in the mirror
and he says what I want him to say.

DÚN AN ÓIR
Golfing Tales from Ceann Sibhéal

1

They were in the throes of building a new course, the furthest west
in Europe. Nine makeshift holes were open and the nineteenth
was a shed. Still I could hire a clutch of clubs and play
to my heart's content for next to nothing while my mother
was catching up with her daily litanies of the dead with friends.
The green-keeper would nod each time I'd pass.

This was a links course for the brave. The rough was a repository
for lost balls. Did I catch up with the dapper gent in front,
dressed casually with care? Or did he catch me? Whichever it was
we played and chatted, kindred spirits getting on, and he'd have
    loved
to play another nine but there were things to do and little time.

Nine holes later I returned the clubs. *Did you enjoy your round
with the Bishop* he enquired, and I was playing the first nine
over again, shot-by-what-was-I-saying-shot.

2

It was another world next time I was over, swish clubhouse
and the ex-policeman to sign me in. And soon enough
we were joined by a couple of latchikos on their seventh
Guinness. A bet it was, then, and we were up with ease
until the world was coming back to them. I had a putt
to win the hole and was readying when the talker of the two
laid a firm hand on my shoulder. *I was wondering
what you were like under pressure,* he said. Men,
I remember thinking, have been murdered for less.

THE END OF GOODBYES
    Murreigh, Easter 1996

Baile na nGall,
Baile cois Abhain,
Baile beag briste,
Lamh le h-uisce,
Agus mna gan tuiscint ann.

                    Ballydavid,
                    House by the river,
                    Small broken house,
                    With the water at hand,
                    And the women who don't understand.

James and Mary

He'd known too many people who
were looking well and they're all dead.
At his age you believe your feet
are carrying you along but they're going
nowhere. He was still translating
from the Gaelic when he spoke,
in tears with Mary, looking for a sign
his sister would remember she'd
been here at all.
            He made me chase
the census man for an English version –
England was a marvellous place with its
money and its education.
                "Qualifications?"
Mary said. "Put that we went to school
and came home again all those years ago."

The Road to Baile na nGall

Was it because we picked up the car
at the airport's edge she thought
it was stolen? It was a long way
to drive, she worried, with the flight
forgotten. Everyone she meets
these days was born in Murreigh –
and she's waiting for James to arrive
from the football sixty years ago,
at eighty-odd and moving
gingerly.
    It wasn't for him
to tell her to get down off the wall
on the road to Baile na nGall with it
not yet dark. He wasn't her father
and it was something she'd not forget.

Maurice

Mother and Maurice were inseparable
until she went to Dublin at seventeen
and he to Chicago. Did he come back
to live alone in this see-through house
beside a nephew who looks out for him,
and the protestant church that lost
its bell, an old witch moving in
who could well be dead?
    We're looking
at a mounted plaque commemorating
thirty years in the City Housing Dept.
and a photograph with colleagues
showing him plumper. He came back
chewing, that's for sure, but he
couldn't be Maurice Malone.

The Monastery

No one remembers the monks but once
this was a convent teeming with nuns.
Now it's a page of windows stuck
on a hill, an advent calendar of its own
demise, the youngest of its six sisters
seventy three. What can Ashe or Collins
do but go on opening their shops?
The auctioneer will come and they'll wait
and see, but God knows who will want
the place with its corridors and rooms.
James thinks it's to do with the telephone
and the outside getting in, like the end
of Latin. And what good could they ever do,
up there on the hill, with their holy lives?

Minard Castle

Stumble on these rocks, imagine
history happening, or at least your mother
in her youth. There were Vikings in the bay,
and Spanish refugees I'm told
we're related to – but Minard's more
modern than you'd think, its fissures
lightning cracks.
        Marian thinks of Brighton
beach blown up a hundred times. She finds
the *Sun* of all things rolled up and wedged
against the wind but Mum stays in the car
with forgotten faces. The holy terrors! Look at them
tripping over these shoe-shine boulders to the sea.
She made the one attempt and all but drowned.
Rain is battering the castle's warning plate.

Gallarus Oratory

Eye of the needle my mother called it
as a girl, the arrow slit they crawled through
out into the fields and away, from the cro,
pre-Christian dry-stone beehive hut.
Over the stile and along the shifting
gravel path (not easy in your seventies)
to a fancy plaque explaining this is
a refined version of what there are still
400 of.
    No chance now of squeezing
through. We laugh about the unfairness
of it all, for we are none of us rich –
but Mum's pre-occupied with a Gaelic
rhyme she's chanting over and over:
Baile na nGall, baile cos abhain …

Bridge and Johnny

No need to be locking the car with the door
of the house wide open. Inside, Bridge is
reeling in the years with Mum who smiles
and leans across to ask "Are you Bridge
Connor?"
    Johnny Griffin's at the door
bellowing through bronchitis, naming
every clutch of houses in the valley and telling
of six in a boat and three canoes for salmon –
two thousand six hundred in two months once,
and a hundred and eleven in one haul!
Now you struggle to catch your breath
but you couldn't forget.
        Tea and barmbrack
and the end of goodbyes and the ride
back repeating "Yes, Mum, that's Bridge."

MORE THAN A MYTH

1

James was failing. So I'd go.
I'd want a car at Shannon.
They'd nothing at the moment
but I was not to worry. They'd see
what they could do when I arrived.
I had no time to wonder what it was
about this uncle I'd hardly seen.

2

They had no car! Another desk,
another company and I was saved,
though I wasn't to think of driving to Dingle
at this time of night. It was after ten.

She smiled. I may have driven there,
but, *believe me, sir,* the roads were worse.
She knew a good hotel close by. A little more
than I would want to pay but comfortable.

3

If I asked nicely I could get a sandwich
in the bar. I've a nice smile I'd tell him later

with a grin. *Indeed, sir, don't I know you do,
but did you get your sandwich?*

4

Breakfast was a roomful of Americans
on pilgrimage, more than fifty of them,
off to Achill Island and the House of Prayer.
They heard that I was here for Uncle James
in hospital, said they'd pray for him.

In the car park stood their luxury coach,
the driver loading luggage into its copious hold.
A rectangular printed card clearly visible
in the front window read: *This vehicle
has been leased to Paul McLoughlin.*

The two of us shook hands laughing
with our other selves – and I was up
and driving in and out of sudden bursts of rain
as if through tunnels. These roads
were not so bad, I thought, until I made it

to Tralee and took an age to go the rest of the way,
bending and twisting and having to park
in a hedge to let the coach pass by
that wasn't about to stop for anyone.

JAMES IS FAILING

James is failing: his eyes, the one ear
he has left, his mind. He wants his dole
and the old coat he'd pull up over himself
before the fire.

     With him, Mary has resisted
all that smacks of complication such as
the recent telephone she picks up only
when it rings. We grew up knowing him
to be contrary and he did throw Marian
out of the house that summer she was there
for drinking a pint at Begley's and missing
early mass for a later one.

But that was our mother's view, herself
motherless in weeks and in the orphanage,
her father unable at work to fend for ten,
then home to find in James the brother who'd
be keeping an eye on her and making sure
she knew she'd to behave.

Mount Brandon rises from the phone box
down in Baile na nGall, enjoys a sky
as cloudless as it gets. Jonjo's round
from behind the hedge to talk, his face
filling the gap left by the passenger window,
lowered electronically, to exchange the time
of day. James was a great man altogether,
forever fashioning something out of nothing.
They talk of him as if he's gone.

He's failing and he's getting worse.
He has a ring of foam to keep one ankle
from the other, bone from bone. They give him
something for the pain, they think it's pain,
he's very agitated, tears the bedclothes
off himself at night, has definitely disimproved.

Al, from Connecticut, loved the hour-long
time-of-days across the gate with James leaning
on the handle of the mower he'd put right
with typical invention. When a big Hausfrau
was wanting to get herself to the other side
of the butter harbour, Smerwick Bay, James
had watched her along the bohareen and mused
she'd only to fall in the water and she'd be there.
There was never an ash out of place in his fire
or a weed in his garden.
          Al lives in the House
of God, after Casadei, his name, but now
he's down the lane helping a friend to fix a wall.
I say it looks hard work. The friend says *Here
we work, we don't work hard, for where's the need.*

The hospital does not announce itself,
might be a school, a run-down smart
hotel. The car park's dual-language sign
informs me where I'll find the Main Entrance,
the Health Centre, Wheelchair Access and
the Mortuary. In the hall a plaque reads
Ospidéal Ceantair An Daingin, the office
unattended, with the men upstairs. The plaque
gives visiting times that no one bothers with.
The men are here to die.

In the ward he twice repeats my name
but doesn't know I'm here. There are other
Jameses and another Jonjo who's whimpering
in his chair. Two nurses haul his featherweight
back into bed, call him *boy*, and then *good man*.
A third arrives to ask if she's been missed,
and when is the mighty dancer to take her out?

Ginger's sitting by his bed, a spread
of photographs behind him on the wall.
He sees me looking at, I think, the proudest son
beside a handsome thoroughbred. A dead horse
he says. Duinin. A grand horse in his time
but now he's dead. And nothing about the boy.
Another's in the corner, propped on pillows,
with the cap over his face and if I lift it up,
I'll get a smile.
      James is eating
barely enough to keep himself alive
and turning that away. He has my arm,
is stroking it and pulling it across the bed
until his breath catches sharply and I'm catching
mine. I squeeze out *James, don't do this to me here.*

GREEN AND GOLD
    for Kathleen

chequered flags are everywhere –
for this is Munster final day.
Men in the ward are confident
despite a nurse's warning
it will never do to be too sure.

You're pleased to see me,
say the game's on in the room
and it's very close – you cannot
watch until the whistle blows.

I work out some at least of the rules,
noticing the runners bounce the ball
alternately on pitch and boot. I know
from somewhere that it's three points
under the bar and one point over.

I open the passenger door for you
and I'm looking pleased because
the nurse had told me if I didn't
they'd be putting me outside
the county boundary.
    You take me
round the lanes to meet my kin,
so many times removed, the kind
my brain cannot accommodate.

And there are cups of tea to greet me
everywhere. It helps the men
have won. Somehow, and distantly,
I'm told I'm something
to O'Sé, the Kerry coach.

THE ROAD TO MURREIGH ('MOOR-EE-UCK')

I knew almost immediately and stopped
to ask a man buried in the boot of his car.
He misheard. *Maria? Is that a person
or a place? A younger, local man emerged:
Murreigh? Well, you could turn back,
but if you keep on down the road,
you'll see a sign.* It's eight kilometres
from Dingle to Murreigh and takes
ten minutes, even on these roads.
But I kept going on the Slea Head Drive.
It took an hour, a meandering,
treacherous ride along the coast
past Ventry Strand, a ninety-degree
turn over stones and running water
at the foot of a cliff until you meet
the shrine that looks out on the Blaskets,
swan-white figures of Christ on his cross,
the blood daubed crimson on his shin
and Mary Magdalene dabbing delicately
at the wounds. They do not judge
the fallen here. It is the will of God.

The road bends north to Dunquin,
its late twentieth-century museum,
the schoolhouse used for *Ryan's Daughter*,
and the jet-black boulders rounded
by sand and by collision with themselves,
some of them fibre-glass added by
the film crew and not retrieved.

Breathtaking views and all the time
in the world but I'd phoned ahead
and they'd be wondering where I was.
What I wanted was a straight road,
not something to admire. I'd seen
my uncle James in the hospital,

grabbed a sandwich in the book-café
and stayed too long, because your man
is exercised by what he's reading
in the Sunday paper. A professor of
psychiatry insists, it says, a little stress
is good for us because without it
life would be forever dull and boring.
Someone asks how could he tell,
for where's the stress in Dingle.
He wants to know is London such
a terrible place, is bothered most
about the air. According to a friend,
it might be many times the size
of Dublin but it's easier to bear
because more organised. I try
to work out what this means, get up
to pay. They ask me what I've had.

Mary, his wife for fifty-one years
and bent double with arthritis,
would be sitting in her chair
to tell me James had been up in the night
to fix the garden – he'd been difficult
and she could not look after him.
Going into Dingle had been his idea.

I'd brought good weather with me;
I should come again. For it was home,
anyway, somewhere that reached down
recovering my mother and the men
gone to America, Matthew and his sons
killed in a boating accident on Lake
Michigan, for Maurice Malone, another
emigré from here, to say it was
the saddest wake he'd ever known,
the three coffins laid out side by side.

James was the only one who stayed,
fishing for crab and lobster, cutting
turf from the bog to feed the fire.
And hanging on with Mary to an old way,
not because he was proselytising
but because he knew it well. He
worried as my mother always did
about what others thought – she
dressed me in first communion white
when we went visiting and panicked
at each playful grubby mark, lest
anyone'd suppose she let me roam.
Whatever we call worry he called life.

I knew when I'd gone wrong and carried on
and recognised the way, how long I'd be
in getting to the house. I'd seen the sights
before. I passed the usual parked cars
and cameras, the binoculars unable to believe
anyone survived on Blasket Island.
But they have not seen James's
face, or Mary's, seen them shy away
from praise, from what they claimed
they didn't understand. To those
who know of it the world looks mad
from here. Looks mad because it is.

Further to the north and east is Ballyferriter,
past a sign for Dún an Óir, the Fort
of Gold, and golf at Sybil Head, until
at last a left turn says *An Mhuirioch*
and I've arrived.

The young man had said if I kept going
down the road I'd see a sign.
If I kept going long enough
I'd see a sign for Rome.

HOLY

There's nothing holy
about Holy Stone
or Holy Ground
except the holes.
   *

Even devotion
at the Holy Well
had pagan origins
to say nothing of
the penny stalls
and other revelries.
   *

The Roman church
came down on patterns,
wiped them clean.
   *

Father Casey broke
the piper and his pipes
and then dispersed
the whole assembly.

Enough for blind Tom
to turn Protestant
with all his songs
and head for Ventry.
   *

Before the Famine
turning Protestant
got you a house
to live in.
   *

In the name of God
there's much that's holy
here but to be sure
you'll find it, look for holes.

THE LONG STICKS

Romeo and Juliet
had their feuding
families shake hands,

hang up the long
sticks they fought with
at the annual fair.

Until the sticks fought
on the wall with no one
wielding them.

Two fathers, civil only
for the sake of both
their houses, now

took down the sticks,
set off for Ballinclare
and beat each other

senseless at the fair.

HANAFIN'S MULE

He was always what we were called
as stubborn as, but the only time
I saw him he was lying in a field,
worn out with age and if he had

a kick left in him it would surely
have finished him off. Seeing him
lying there didn't make me want
to go in and chance my arm

only for the adults to say wasn't I
the very incarnation of the mule,
the number of times I'd been told
and them wasting their breath,

for Hanafin's Mule was Hanafin's
Mule and if you'd an ounce of sense
you'd keep your distance. None
but a fool would be wasting his time

if the mule's answer was no.

THE BED AND BREAKFAST HISTORY MAN

She wonders does he have an iron.
He does, he says, of course, then wonders
if he does and where the thing might be
until he stumbles on a plug and follows it.

His daughter races in and wonders loudly
does anyone have sixty teeth. Of course,
he tells her. Dinosaurs. People, she says.
But he's explaining local place-names

to a guest he's just made breakfast for,
insisting that whoever it was suggested
the crack in Minard Castle was the work
of lightning put them wrong for sure.

He has a heavy, loping tread, parks
his Golf and trailer against the wall so close
you'd struggle to slip a couple of pages
of the *Irish Times* into the gap.

He's on the mantelpiece with his degree
in archaeology and, yes, he does the tours
in summer. It was Oliver Cromwell, all right.
There isn't a doubt about that.

DUNQUIN

These rocks might be the flukes
of dolphins cursed re-entering
the sea by locals fearing further
blight or famine or disease.

Just look at them, involuntary
interlopers, pop-up targets, forcing
a violence of waves unfathomably
over and over to divide to rule,

to take its fury out on Clogher Head
in the inter-continental wake of
Brendan, *discoverer of America,*
whatever the Spanish might say.

It is said the kingdom is lost
to those who look on it alone,
that you need a loving companion
with you to experience the pain

and hurt of beauty, to get the *real*
feel of the ocean, take in a sky
that shifts from gold to stippled
azure to a requiem of purple.

But it looks real and mythical
enough to me, less than a blow-in,
coming here for death to bring
my mother home and now

for James, to watch breakers
crash against volcanic cliff,
like a strop brought down
to teach a boy his manners,

cliffs that cannot run away
to England to find work or
peace. Nor may the growing
boys, for all's erosion now,

the jobs dried up, the old ways
flukes in an uncomprehending
sea of targets to be met,
not fired at, a world apart

that Brendan stumbled on,
a progress no one recognised,
written on the sky he left
behind, a death still happening.

THE LAST
for Maureen

He walks in his big coat
on the road from Ballydavid
and a drink while you
clamber along the cliff
in search of the old road
claimed by the sea.

The nurse lit a candle, placed it
at the foot of his bed, started,
softly, to say the rosary. By
the third Gaelic Hail Mary
you knew the words.

No more fire or the oil lamps
lighting the place or the smell
across the way of the shoe
as it hissed. No more
the women off to the well
with buckets for the time of day.

From what remains of the old
road you watch the sea
where James and all the
fishermen bring in their boats.

When he died, the candle
frizzled out. You wonder
was the room shrinkwrapping
his life.

STORIES BY THE FIRE

I. James

It was regular as clockwork,
cutting across the fields
at dawn to meet the fishermen,

until as usual we climbed the fence
and Patrick froze. I saw nothing,
let alone some fella in a ditch.

He locked himself away at home,
heard father pronounce the man
the owner of the field and dead

these fifteen years. He wasn't right
from that day on and people say
it's why he died so young and on

the feast day of the man he saw.
In the pitch dark all sorts look alive
or dead and doesn't everyone

dress more or less the same?
No one questioned Elizabeth,
our sister, feeling a clipped ear

from his hand in the night,
for mumbling she was too tired
to get up to our ailing father's call.

II. Maureen

The four of us girls with only
a torch between us, set off
for the Liss high up by Ballydavid
Head to test the truth of it,

that on the stroke of midnight
O's and Mc's can hear
the banshee there. With icy breath
we ringed the grassy hollow,

shone the torch down into it,
to face a pair of bright eyes
staring up at us. Needless to say
the creature began to bleat.

It made us bold enough
to clamber down and sing
and dance a manic jig –
till out of the darkness

came a cry so pitiful
we couldn't scream
and the thing appeared,
a ghostly apparition,

Mossy O'Connor, eldest
son, pulling at the sheet
he'd gathered round himself
and laughing himself insane.

Toward dawn, somehow
it's always dawn, he was
shivering along with us –
and even now is never sure.

DINGLE NIGHTCAP

Somewhere quiet, away from the busier bars
and the noise. *Oh, that'll be us,* the barmaid sighs

and I'm into one of the corners with a pint
to browse the bookshelves' sleeveless offerings:

'Kerly's Law of Trade Marks and Trade Names',
Osgood's 'Functions of Real and Complex Variables'.

Afterwards I skirt the stream that set the visitor
from Dublin in a spin – Look at the way it flows

under the buildings, there! – and vexed his
little ones who'd somewhere pressing else to go.

I turn the key and creep upstairs for fear I'll wake
a living soul. Someone's breathing belches

in the dead of night. Tomorrow I will pick up
speed for Shannon, head back to a study lined

with other books, arrive with culture-lag,
convince myself I'd not survive here long.

The hostess, as she calls herself, now
has a credit-card machine she bullies

till it locks. She tends the pretty garden
and her reach of stream that's travelled all the way

from Connor Pass. What with everything else
it keeps her busy till October time.

CRÓ NA SNÁTHAIDE*

1

The procession passes the house
with Mary at the kitchen window
looking out. She'd seen him
at the funeral home looking awful
pale and cold. Mind you, she said,
you would be when you're dead.

2

You take the short walk
to the table and the
long walk to the grave,
the coffin hoisted high
on sturdy shoulders.

3

The men take up the long-handled shovels
to fill the grave. It's many a time I've taken
a shovel with James. God, he was good
with the shovel, like everything else. The
women stand aside with James's flowers.

4

This was a beautiful place
to be buried, with the mountains behind
and the sweep of the harbour in front.
You get a better look at it standing
than when you're lying in the grave.

5

The church at Kilmalkedar's
in ruins save the eye of the needle,
the long, narrow window at the far end.
If you can go through the window
and back three times, then luck
will be with you. If you're stuck
and unable to pass you'll go
to Hell. The fear of mortal sin
can weigh you down.

(* *Cró na Snáthaide:* eye of the needle)

BALLYLUSKEY
for Caitlín

Through Carraige and before Feohanagh,
the windy place, find Ballyluskey, painted
on a roadside wall of rock. The path
I always think I'll miss winds round until
a tight left turn into your yard. I'm used to it,
my fourth time of visiting over the years,
though now I venture beyond the kitchen
in search of photos of you and my mother,
who was always in the middle of the fun.

You'd visit her in Acton with Dad gone
to the army and you'd need a stay-out pass.
Nurses were forever under lock and key.
You'd earned your place in England
but it was two years only before
you were back to care for your mother.
The modern world is easier and you're quick
to laugh. I have a couple of snaps of you
and Nina – it's her first time here,
if you don't count Dublin, and no one does.

Huge smiles as if you're back together
again at last. The photographs of you
and Mum are nowhere to be found. So
they'll be somewhere else. You make sure
to sprinkle holy water on us when we leave.

KILMALKEDAR

We stumbled between graves,
trying not to stand on any.

There are no Ashes left
in a place that once was full of them,

and none here that we could see.
I was giving up the ghost

when the woman who'd parked up
asked who would I be and *Which James Ashe?*

and showed the way. They're here
as Seamus and Máire Áġas.

Out of the drizzle, in Lord Baker's for a drink –
we'd eaten there the night before –

the barman told a couple in the corner
who we were and why we'd come.

*And you were up at the cemetery
not an hour ago*, the woman said,

the sister of the one who'd put us right.
Mary'd been a family godmother.

If here you don't watch what you do,
then others will. It must be so.

SAFETY FIRST

Cars slow but press on not wanting to be beaten
by a black-and-white mutt and not wanting
to run it down. When the game subsides,
cars move on beyond an incident their drivers
won't recall until the next jolt while the dog
finds a roadside bush to mark as its own,
careful to keep its head stuck out for all to see.

It must be used to cars, must dice with dodgems
when it can, was born into what, at school,
we usually took some time to learn — how
never to be the person no one knew was there.

CLARKE'S WINDOWS
Presentation Convent Chapel, Dingle

Heresy, I suppose, preferring Donatello
to Michelangelo, a life lived, his Mary Magdalene,
to the perfect form. Here women old enough
know the hard life for accepting how things are,
and letting the men who wait for everything
to be in front of them go on believing they're in charge.

Look at Clarke's women looking to anything but
the men: the crone with no teeth and a world
of troubles on her shoulders and the many who must
turn to joining threads for the loom and binding oats
and milking evil-tempered cows. Their faces know
there's nothing to be done. They look to the future
wearing Russian hats and exotic costumes.

It's what art can do. While Christ endures
Gethsemane as if the pain were disappointment
that his people should behave this way and not
the rack of torture. He left the agony behind.
Were David here and real he'd be forever in the gym.

LEST

There are simple truths:

that my mother had a life before me,
knew how to enjoy herself, was innocent
of what she did, would not be blamed;

that we all came with a pint of Guinness
to a house that would have loved
a son a priest but didn't press,

in which she'd giggle uncontrollably
at Dad in underpants, leaving us
to grow up knowing stomach cramps

but not that we could fart; that I was dressed
in white when visiting to show
the slightest speck lest any think her bad;

that without a mother she was farmed out
early to the Heights from a house
of ten with her father off out after work;

that what's revisited is changed,
even when you weren't there at the time
and all you know is by report;

that James was funny and cantankerous,
his mischief-making finding fault
with those he'd never hurt,

for if you insult one out here,
you insult them all, the gift of a poem
locked away lest any read it wrong

in a world of lest and saying nothing
to the priest, the man of God,
who mightn't be much of a man at all,

of saying nothing to anyone
could it be borne and even when it couldn't
for all the good it would do;

that what you do see changes –
where was it I read about lightning cracks?
and where are the shiny black rocks?

that with James gone they'd build the bridge
he'd never hear of across the stream
and there'd appear a planning application

on the gate; that the place would be
falling down without
his being here and making do;

that my mother thought him the most
contrary man ever to put shoes on his two feet,
when I thought he made us all better;

that there are simple truths,
the ways of things that will not change,
that disappear.

from

The Hungarian Who Beat Brazil (2017)
Whatever Else You Might Say (2021)
Uncollected Poems (2018–21)

MANTLES

Googling the place draws a blank,
the electrical retailer's I stood for hours in the entrance of
till Godfrey Evans took a catch and the screen went dead.
Once when the owner, Mr Ewing, asked if I wanted a chair,
I said yes, please, but it never appeared.

I trailed after Dad when he went in search of Magpies
playing someone or other in a 50s' Cup Final, ending up
in the local Co-Op basement with a fair old crowd,
till the manager pulled the plug on us.
Did we still have gas mantles then, those gossamer-thin
pre-electric bulbs it was my job to stand on a chair and replace
when they'd had their chips? There'd be trouble in store

if they laddered. Ewings had radiograms, sturdy bits
of furniture on spindly legs, along from the newsagent's,
The Dolls Hospital, where I bought the *Tiger*
from a trestle table in the street with a box for the money.

It was dark inside. Once when I ventured in
(was there not enough change?) and walked down the aisle
to the counter that stood at the back in the gloom,
a bubbly bloke in a rush (he'd left his engine running)
was asking Mr Davies if he'd any dirty books.
No one in his right mind'd go back there.

TWO-O-EIGHT

I'd listen to Radio Luxembourg,
could it have been the same time
every night, (or once a week),
to a fifteen minute top ten show
that featured *Sea of Heartbreak*
for what seemed like ever?

The Everly Brothers' *Cathy's Clown*
(the one-hundred-and-forty-ninth
greatest song of all time) had been
the UK Number One for seven weeks,
so it must have been a C & W chart,
and I've always hated Country –

how can bass players stand those
simple first and third beats,
tonic-dominant, all night long?
I'd endure the nasal women
and the men's deep-throated treacle
for Don Gibson's song, again and again.

It was something to do with his voice,
the literate progress of the harmony,
the veering off into the hook
and a foreshortened bridge.
Whatever it was, the thing
survived its classification.

Why else would I have listened
every night (or was it once a week)
for a song about a lonely ship at sea?

BROTHERS
for Peter Rostron

The Brothers would have none of Satan's lyrics
within their walls, allowable recordings
being strictly instrumental, heaven only knowing
what itsy-bitsy teeny-weeny yellow polka-dot
bikinis might do to adolescent minds,
and did on visits home. Boots Randolph was
a way of smuggling in the devil's chords.

We can still hear missionaries belching out
the hellfire godless readers might suppose
was James Joyce on a roll. Shedding the skin
it burnt took time we'd all have better spent
on growing up. Cruelty seemed no more
than we deserved, resentment turning
inwards, having nowhere else to go.

At lunch Ollie boasted about skipping
Sunday Mass, so he was doubly damned.
Tines were for spearing peas, and absolutely
not for shovelling them up like coal
the colour of our souls. Did we believe
such guff, even then? It can't have been
indoctrination. Somehow we squirmed
into a fog of sub-Damascan light.

Now, we wouldn't let Boots Randolph
in the house, preferring Norwich's
festival with Branford Marsalis in a church
or the wondrous sax of a cathedralled
Andy Sheppard cantata premiered
with a conductor whose dancing baton
caught uneven time and a choir intent
on nailing his post-modern groove.

SUNDAYS

It's tempting to suppose that no one goes
to church save queens and ministers, that Donne
would have his sermons broadcast in surround
sound to the vortex of near-empty pews,

that things disintegrate because the young
can never see the point of what they're told
they'll understand in time – say, that you can't
swap God for the fripperies of shopping,

that closing cinemas and football grounds
was rooted in good family sense, that the
Lord must have his day. Why so? It's tempting
to suppose the set-in-stone must be unsound.

Traffic crawls. Finals are played. The shops
dare not stay closed. But who'd return to Dad
taking a month of them to cut your hair
the way you hate, and nothing to do all day?

WANT

Sunday lunch was perfect. He was never
going to see my disappointment in him,
nor did I want him to. I lost it every time.
He was our first. We make mistakes.
My time was taken up in finding work.

He got to grammar school without much
help from us. I left at twelve, his mum at ten.
And then he messed with boxing, won things,
got put down a class. I wanted to be proud
and for a while I was. None of us

made anything of school. And he was
wasting it, this chance to get away
from what we had. I knew a man who'd
grown up on the border whose father
clipped him round the ear for playing cricket.

When we were in W3 I was banned
from many a house for keeping such stuff
from my kids. I didn't want them
growing up to bite the hand that fed them.
Was I wrong?

I bought him a smart hard-wearing jacket
from Ravilious. He wore a Beatles' jacket,
grew his hair. None of this should matter
but he wouldn't see. All he wanted
was to hold his own. I died too young.

I was left with what might have been.
After the war we could have bought a house
for next to nothing when even that was hard
to find and we'd have owned the place.
But she said no. It's all she ever said.

THE HUNGARIAN WHO BEAT BRAZIL
   for my father (1918–1980)

What we were at one about was
the Hungarian who beat Brazil.

He quickened hearts each time
he touched the ball or quickened

ours, and his death invited
obituarists to note no more

than those who saw him
would expect: his elegance,

his close control, his poise,
his Ballon d'Or. For you

he was a dancer with the ball
tied to his boot; the way he'd

glide. He floated over grass
like a human hovercraft, you said.

It wasn't just the guile, the finishing,
the grace that made us all forget

the missing Pele. It was
that movement in the gut

that followed Albert running rings round
brawn and brilliance, the turning

to whoever was beside you,
known or not, to smile. Some

see poise as tippy-tappy
weakness, the dour brigade,

but the one thing we agreed on,
recovering from another Sunday row

when silence was the aftermath
and balls were neither here nor there,

we'd rather Albert floated into view
than someone scything Pele at the knee.

i.m. Florian Albert (1941–2011)

THE END OF EMPIRE
Chiswick Empire 1912–1959

In '57 Lonnie Donegan was Wishy-Washy until a programme insert
told us he was indisposed, so the claim I saw him in Aladdin
became a lie I almost believed in the end. Liberace
brought the final full house down in '59 and Empire House
    went up,
an office block. Why the council sold was a mystery even then.

I only had to look out of my bedroom window to see who was on
next week: Alma Cogan in the tallest headline letters, down
through middling Dave King to the small fry whose lettering
rarely grew. Colours were wishy-washy but that poster
was our road's top of the bill after the fire engines' red next door.

I loved it when the man in overalls arrived with his rolls and paste
and ladder. He'd manoeuvre every hang until you couldn't see
the joins, even if you stood up close. Cogan sang a song
about a chicken and died at 34. Perhaps the Empire would've
collapsed on its own and someone on the council knew.

No one in a boy band's heard of the place, but there are Sikhs
round here who cannot name the five Ks, let alone tell you
about the Raj. Miles Davis must've seen what was coming
after '67, playing Hammersmith then going electric
before the Odeon changed its name, then changed it back again.

It's how things work, the ripple from a flung stone till the waters
smooth themselves, like someone ridding a skirt of crumbs.

HOUSE
Thoughts after Rachel Whiteread

The final occupant vacates the premises,
moves out or on, to disappear or flourish
somewhere else, the house turned inside
out when cast in concrete, to be noisily
destroyed when finally adjudged an eyesore
and denied the anonymity of crumbling
silently. Pigeons sculpted in the dust
of windows by Mondrian are indifferent
to what may be inside or may have been.

Building going on around him everywhere,
Maurice sits on under blankets in his chair,
watching time go by and letting it. Sometimes
I see him exploded into particles in time
to make the evening news, with James and Ellen
telling disbelieving viewers we're to pay
no heed to him. It's only what they would
have said from fear they might be blamed
for the catastrophe, or any part of it.

IN PRAISE OF DRAB

Drab does not reveal itself
immediately and its bum
is never pinched.

Drab walks on stilts
occasionally for sport
but eschews stilettos.

Drab serves a purpose
other than itself, its mirror
making sure it's not absurd.

Drab gets where it wants to go
unnoticed if it can
by being not too drab.

Drab does not dress
for God or other drabs
but keeps what's inside in.

Drab would not be seen
dead on a catwalk
nor in a rainbow.

Drab's a cheerful study
in brown that chooses
not to smile aloud.

Drab ignores
the grosser insults,
objects to being

simply dull or simply
anything, remains
a positive opaque.

Drab cleaves
to a quiet life, is not ashamed
to put net curtains up.

Drab's different
when you get to know it,
comes out of itself.

Drab's full
of surprises, leaves
a lot to be desired.

DYING OUT

The seal's harpooned
with floats then dead
from a single rifle-shot.

It will be butchered
expertly past midnight,
its skin housing meat

like arctic haggis.
The man who killed it
dangles from a three-man

hand-held nylon rope
raiding hundred-metre
drops for guillemot eggs.

Alert and stressed
he sometimes thinks
the cliff alive, his flung

rock missing (just)
the cameraman forgotten,
snugly harnessed, gob-

smacked, feet below.
He'll turn down a korma,
stick to his seal, its

intestine the producer
judging less disgusting
than he'd thought.

ENDS MEET

Every time I need a new white good, I add
an extended warranty to see me through until
the thing needs replacing. It's called wealth-creation,
from which we all benefit, a form of mutual aid.

The man in Westminster knows what's good for me
better than I do because he knows what's good. His
name is Gideon but someone told me he believed it
more unlikely he'd be blamed if he changed it to George.

So he did. It's only recently got out. I don't know why.
His department sent me ten pounds as a present
and a hundred pounds for winter fuel. It's getting
easier. Gideon's to do with bibles. It's a good name.

RITUAL
for Brian Jones (1938–2009)

1 L'église Saint-Ouen, Pont-Audemer

Killing time, I happen on the mass I knew
in Latin as an altar boy, loving its sound.
Here, in another foreign tongue, its cant
is lost again to choreography, the host held up
to murmur and let melt. Voices flattered
by a kind acoustic sing in unison. It is
beyond all thought. Your search for purpose
took you otherwhere. There is no God.

But there is history, this imposing mass,
its lantern tower, the bridge by Odomar
that gave the place its name, things to admire,
while communicants stand with their priest
in prayer. When you were a child and real,
you lay up on your tar roof itching for the world.

2 Chambre Funéraire

I visit churches now, not minding
being taken back like this to stare
at habit and desire. When this place

was not to be the capital, they left it
incomplete. Why bother finishing
what would only ever be a shell?

We shall dress informally, place
single flowers carefully, look lost.
How far you've grown since Islington.

Back inside our cars we'll follow.
Burning is unusual in France.
Religion holds its ground in *cimtières*

3 Yvetot Crematorium

From here we cannot feel the wind
the trees outside are dancing to, though
they'd be dancing anyway to any air,

and there is no lark rising in conditioned air –
the funeral director got the music wrong.
You'd have smiled and played the error down

for what it's worth. Words are mattering.
The known may soften blows for some,
but you'd have had us start again each time.

There is a film next door that shows a box
slide by on rails. It happens slowly very fast.
You knew we'd look on looking at ourselves.

LOOKING FOR THE BOSTON LOWELL

Snowy Washington's a plane-hop to a seriously sub-zero Boston.
I'd lost my cap of twenty years (from Firenza) at DC's Library
      of Congress,
the entrance to its Extension Building blocked by a smiling guard
who'd never heard of Robert Lowell (or the recording of him
      reading
in the 70s) and directed me to the Gift Shop in the (right)
Jefferson Building as if there were a chance of finding it there.

The woman at the Information Desk (who hadn't heard of
      Lowell either)
couldn't recall (when I returned) my wearing a cap. She was sure.
By the time I was half way down Independence I was convinced
I'd find it on its hook at home. She'd said I might look for the
      record.
online, but, yes, I could be anywhere for that.

So I went through New Year in San Francisco and San Jose
and for a further couple of days back in DC bare-headed.
But Boston was another matter. Going the wrong way first,
looking for Little Italy we found Salem Street and, two doors in,
the greatest hat shop my little world had ever seen. I bought
a brand new gift-wrapped cap and a woolly hat to pull down
over my frozen ears, and I was ready for anything.

Except the PUBLIC LIBRARY opposite Trinity Church
by the BOYLESTON street-sign (there are Lowell prompts
everywhere, like the Shaw Memorial relief obscured by TV
scaffolding and a cameraman who was waiting for the newly-elected
governor to emerge from the State House, and like everyone
      else we met,
had never heard of Lowell). The library's open to everyone.
      Look it up.
Pop your head inside the silent reading rooms (without a seat
      to be had)
and tell me there isn't hope for the world now my ears are warm.

PAST PASSING
    Horace: Epistles I (i)
    (for John Forth)

You once asked what had happened to
the bloke who'd written this, and this, and this ...
Too busy bending to the world's will, mate,
to be engaged in stuff like poetry and jazz,
an anarchic soul who would be left alone.
Too busy failing to get on, more like.

I picked up pen and horn again, reminded
virtue is a friend who twists your arm.
(A girlfriend said I wore it like a badge.)

Things change and stay the same, we all know that.
We grow up in an age we learn to live in
till its gone and we're admired for what's
eluded us. The young are all for change
yet look for wisdom in the lives of those
still living who have lived, at least a bit.

It isn't enough, of course, but it will
have to do. Staying among the unrelated
young shows us there's always stuff to like.

GONE & DONE

1. (Thomas)

Gall goyne is your pronouncement
on an empty bowl,
your shoulders pinched,
your palms pushed out before you
like the Pope.

All gone. So were the seventies,
almost, at your birth,
your grandad said –
whose heart gave out when you were
less than one.

Father Pat spoke movingly
of love and loss,
leading us
through decade after decade
of the rosary.

You push your plate away
long before knowing
the names of things,
and articulate their absence
with a grin.

2. (Niamh)

Palms up, it's a first word
for what's over and done with
like food – and time to be hoicked
out of your high-chair to put
everything back in the tin
you'd empty it from. No big deal
but what's so. When we cleared
two rooms for the decorators
including seven floor-to-ceiling
bookcases emptied of books
and filled again, one by one,
then back again, that too
was done and so were we.
But the books that went
to the charity shop or the dump
or a mate who didn't have that one,
that wasn't done, that was pain.
The study's a study in neatness now,
it boasts an armchair and a plant,
and all the books are on shelves,
and those about books I'll never
teach again had little answer
to any palms-up insistence
that what's done is done.

THE CHILL PILL

It bothered me not being able to strike irons
properly, and (temporarily) losing things
I never used to lose; or that two bare-topped
teenagers kept up middle-of-the-road wheelies
ignoring a futile honk or two from behind;

that educated people went on willfully
misrepresenting what others said
to suit themselves; or that suddenly
everything was iconic or robust or a scenario
and like was like a fashion accessory
for more than those who'd affected vocal fry,
not because they have anything to do
with language moving on but because
they're lazy locutions and clubs to join …

Since I've been taking the pill, however,
the aforesaid (and much more of the same),
no longer bother me, which bothers me
more than all the others put together. The
far from empty tub is, therefore, enclosed.

DON CHERRY
A photograph by Ole Brask – Jazz People (New York: Abrams, 1976)

He's clutching his leather, weather-beaten case with
its puffed out cheeks to his chest as anyone might
his name. Inside's the trumpet he's creating it with.

He's on a platform looking leisurely down and
away from Grand Central's tracks, his wool-trimmed jacket
half-unzipped over collared shirt and crew-neck jumper,

casually well-turned out, relaxed, his hair well-groomed.
Jazz is moving on. Let critics argue over
how good he is, the missed/muffed notes on runs at speed

against the tight and twisting ingenuity
of his inventing that's determined to avoid
a tonal centre. Nothing new in this – Schoenberg

and Webern got there first – but like them Cherry
from his youthful days with Ornette on can still sound
mega-new. How long before the new sounds old?

And as for 'free', avoiding tonal centres sounds
like a solid rule to me. But he stuck with it
all his life on his way to the Oklahoma

Hall of Fame, which might not sound like much.
His influences include a host of household
names we're had to believe but listen for yourself.

He's on a platform waiting and we know something
of what happens. There's another further along from
him with a straight-edged attaché case and a third

in a raincoat looking glum. Who we know nothing of.
It's a platform of speed-stripes at rest. We all board
trains to get perhaps where we were always going.

HOW CAPITALISM WORKS
i.m. Bertie Lomas, who wanted to be remembered for his treatise
– Who Needs Money? (Blond & Briggs, 1972)

We all know the mechanic's sharp
intake of breath, and that paying
for taxis is cheaper than running a car;

that there's more than enough food
in the world to feed everyone,
and deep down that money

is unnecessary, its absence revealing
what matters to us; and that if
we didn't have to pay for anything

having more of it than we need
would be ridiculous, so the complaint
of those with shedloads of the stuff,

that we shouldn't want to go back to
bartering, would be equally ridiculous
as there's no evidence of a barter system

existing anywhere ever. We also know
that motor insurers are legalized crooks
who've persuaded governments

they can't take risks. All this, and yet
I know the sound of a Maserati
as it glides slowly by. It isn't a growl

or a purr but a deeply satisfied hum.

IN OTHER WORDS

Know-alls worth their salt
hearing it feels like someone
sitting on your chest will say
'Heart' immediately.
And be right, of course.

Cardiac enzymes are proteins
released into the system
as and when. They warn.
In other words an injured
heart is flagging up a heavy
workload: Get testing now.

It's no accident medicine's
still in Latin. Gut's no use
if you want it fixed. Too
imprecise. And everybody's
well aware of stuff like that
even if unable to itemize.

We all just hope the doctors
can. Though increasingly
the doctors are ignored until
they can't be. Know-alls
have metamorphosed
into entitlements

with clipboards. Me, I
surrender to what's happening,
knowing I can't fix myself.
Stuff your fears about intrusion.
On the anaesthetist's trolley
I'd recover or I wouldn't.

'IT'S RESPECT FOR THE FUCKING DEAD'
– *Royal Engineers' sergeant major*

With my parents over for Sunday lunch
our front-room door jammed tight shut
and Mum of course decided she needed the loo
and Dad asked didn't we have a toolbox.
I looked down from our first-floor flat
to see Graham, a neighbour's teenage son,

    walking up the path on his way home
    so I called down asking him to get into
    our kitchen from the fire-escape the
    estate agent had called a parapet
    breaking a window pane in the door
    if he had to, and come to our rescue.

But, Graham, we have my parents here
so you cannot, must not swear. He
nodded since he couldn't speak –
he couldn't let a noun go by – sometimes
he'd split a word in two, tell us
the film was fan-fucking-tastic.

He rescued us in silence without
breaking any glass and left nodding
all the way down stairs with thanks
ringing in his ears. He joined the army
which you'd expect and when he came out
he didn't swear which you wouldn't.

TO WHOM IT MAY CONCERN

Flowers bunched and wrapped
congregate round lamp posts,
next to railings, outside a home.
You see them from your car,
glimpsed and gone or stared at
when you're at lights or in a jam.
Some are expensive bouquets,
rarely anything as cheap as pinks
or alstroemeria though both
regularly cheer the place up
where I live. As if the more you
spend the more you care. What
occasioned these post-life
flowerings is invariably sad
or shocking and reminds us
of our own misfortunes
and what we know and love
but they're little if anything
to do with those who've lost
whoever it is the flowers
commemorate. They are
a public joining-in, unsought,
with private grief. I drive on
wanting no such flowers for me.

NO ORDINARY CLIPPER

I'll come clean. No one's taking
anyone back to any nineteenth-century
Thermopylae – Cutty Sark race
more or less voided when the joy
of Greenwich lost a rudder and
murmured home seven days late
with its proverbial sails between
its legs leaving its rival with its
three pillowed tower-blocks
and a Pyrrhic victory the Greeks
wouldn't have wanted anything
named after let alone a tea clipper
later sold to Portugal for use as
a naval training ship and renamed
the Pedro Nunes (or Nunez) before
being torpedoed at sea off Cascais
in 1907; mine's by Whittard of
Chelsea and yesterday I clipped it
and chipped it as I was loading
the dish washer. It's no laughing
matter. I've had it years, use it
every morning I'm here and
replacing it may not be easy.
How long I can go on looking
at the tab of white where the chip
once was remains to be seen…

WANTED

Selling poetry's a niche art we'd love you to try your hand at.
Language is important. Begin the pitch with Dear Poetry Fans
or Lovers, as you wish. You're putting poetry out there,
on the streets, which best suits buoyant adjectives and verbs.
So here's a list of likelies: events are not to be missed
because the poems and their poets are amazing, fabulous,
exciting, inspirational, and always great. Depending on your
target audience you might find room for diverse, eclectic,
subtle, even imaginative. All poems and their poets are to be
celebrated, otherwise there is no point. Their work is dazzling
or it's nothing. Vloggers please note that vocal fry's a seller,
and if your brief extends to exegeses (though you shouldn't
even think of using such a word) make sure they're interspersed with words like beautiful and brilliant without
straying far from anything learnable from the University
of the Bleedin' Obvious. Smile and enthuse, of course,
to make the old farts hate you, and remember at all times
and at all cost you are writing about poems, so be careful
not to look or sound like one. Just aim to persuade those
who love what's very poetic to attend so they can wait
until each poem ends before exhaling an orgasmic 'Ah'.

OVERNIGHTING

Romantics scribble gibberish on cuffs
including what they like to think inspired;
classicists put what glisters in a drawer
and let it soak to show itself as tired

and not worth persevering with – or
even better than they thought at first.
But even ancients knew that sometimes
it's as well to let things do their worst.

What soaks can fester, we all know that!
But letting soak can be a respite
from what's flying past, time to read again,
secure with someone who can write!

And letting soak can be like having
a trusted editor, someone who knows
your foibles and can temper what you say,
can fire up what your passions froze

or dampen what it's wise to have put out.
Soaking for me means overnighting
porage oats. Does it really these days
amend both taste and breakfast writing?

THE PIER VISITOR EXPERIENCE MANAGER

Ruth's fifty and five foot nothing and more
than a match for most things short of tying up
the boat that's coming in unexpectedly with
its hobbler set in the pub and refusing to budge.

She wants to work in *Asda* until we tell her
she'll have to leave the staff area walking
past a sign that blazons 'Smile, You're On
The Asda Stage'. *Waitrose,* then, she says.

Leaving the pier with their post-post-grad son
a couple stop to say thanks and the well-past-
sixty mother tells Ruth she's glad someone else
likes turquoise, the colour of the former's

chiffon scarf and the latter's dress. Ruth tells her
she looks very beautiful and there are smiles
all round. Once they leave, I sort of agree
but say I could have done without the white

translucent see-through dress advertising her
knickers. The poor woman, Ruth exclaimed,
hoping desperately she can't have known,
though I wasn't sure. Inside the entrance-shop

Ruth suddenly lifts her skirt to reveal the also-
turquoise almost knee-length leggings
underneath. I buy the brochure that tells me all
about the pier and its history of being loved.

SHEPP
for Peter Rostron

It's not about jazz, but reducing us cynics to tears.
He's a little late on, a worry at his age, but the bass and piano,
the youngsters, are out with a bounce. Even then, a pause,

time to fret some more before he shuffles past the piano
in carpet slippers and settles in the magisterial velvet chair
he'll play the set from, an odd-shaped soprano he'll ignore

laid out on his cushioned table like an open-mouthed golden
fish on ice, his embouchure enough to give a teacher fits,
a beaver breaking water for the lower registers, a baby

battling with a teat when he's further up – but no matter
where he is in his torrent of notes you hardly see his fingers
move, their tips barely touching the keys it seems.

He takes a hit-and-miss age to clip sax-sling to horn,
and longer to find the cap to his silver tenor in his pocket
and sheathe the mouthpiece with it, with us wondering why,

till he's on his feet singing how He Don't Get Around Much
No More, Ellington's toon and Dook would have loved it.
The knowing smiles of the Conservatory-trained piano
and bass tell us they're constantly amazed at every switch.

I tell our attentive waiter this is my best night at Ronnie's
since Roland Kirk (before he was born) when Stevie Wonder
came on with his mouth organ and wowed even Kirk.

The 'support' band that night was Harold McNair,
who was so good I wanted to be him. Kirk had to be seen
in the flesh and heard with your own ears live. Like Shepp.

TURNING HANDS
for Marcus

Yours, devoid of nostalgia? Are you sure
it's not a case of preferring to stay
homesick rather than having to endure

being home, a case of seizing the day
as if there were a way of finding
in seizure the very food of life? Instead,

you find yourself having to eat words
you thought were anyway crude
just to make it through. Nostalgia

may ring seldom true but at least
its mainspring hints at roots,
the absence of which kept vexing

wandering wodwos trying to make sense
of who or what or even why they were
and thinking life a queer coincidence

of moving on. What takes you back can stir
the promise of history's imperfect cure
which is all we've got, and is everywhere.

THE TWENTIETH CENTURY*

People saw in it an avenue
dark, unnamed and endless;
doomed and domed experiments,
and scattered points-of-light.

A bayonetter ran listening
between footfalls for the
reason of his still running,
and Wodwo went on looking,

while low, dishonest men
murdered sleep in others
if not themselves. Dry
economics slunk off

with some of what was left
in the wake of post-this-that
tyrannies that tortured thought,
forgot the people in them, leaders

worshipping banality and detail,
the century's new gods – and someone
somewhere found in all of this
a little of the marsh in naming it.

(* with due acknowledgement to Edward Thomas, Eliot, Auden, Ted Hughes, Brian Jones and Mark Doty)

WHAT THEY WERE GOOD AT

When the armies marched back
their leaders assumed
things would go back to normal –
but normal had changed
for good, or what seemed
at the time like good.

When the women came back
the men were anxious
wondering whether the boardroom
would still be theirs
or whether they'd have to resume
what they were good at.

Children had grown accustomed
to life without mothers,
to being grown up,
and if they could help it,
mothers would have to get used
to how things were now.

It was uncomfortable
for a long while. There
was enough anger
and crowing and ladying it
to feed an army
so that when the armies

had to march off again
the war they were off
to fight in seemed not like
a war at all except that
people still died, but that
hardly seemed the point.